CONFLICTING LOYALTIES

My Life as a Mob Enforcer Turned DOJ Informant

AIDEN GABOR

Skyhorse Publishing

Editor's Note:

Names, dates, and places have been changed to protect the guilty.

Skyhorse Publishing books may be purchased in bulk at special discounts for sales promotion, corporate gifts, fund-raising, or educational purposes. Special editions can also be created to specifications. For details, contact the Special Sales Department, Skyhorse Publishing, 307 West 36th Street, 11th Floor, New York, NY 10018 or info@skyhorsepublishing.com.

Skyhorse® and Skyhorse Publishing® are registered trademarks of Skyhorse Publishing, Inc.®, a Delaware corporation.

Visit our website at www.skyhorsepublishing.com.

10 9 8 7 6 5 4 3 2 1

Library of Congress Cataloging-in-Publication Data is available on file.

Cover design by David Ter-Avanesyan
Images from Shutterstock

ISBN: 978-1-5107-7967-9
Ebook ISBN: 978-1-5107-7968-6

Printed in the United States of America

CHAPTER 1

The diagnosis was a death sentence.

A night nurse pushed my wheelchair down a crowded white hallway. Parked me in a cold exam room. She turned on the light and prepped the MRI. My stomach turned at the stink of hospital gauze. I wanted to go home. I wanted to start over. She took my temperature and blood pressure and jotted some notes. Then she helped me stand. Eased me onto the scanner bed.

We were on the third floor of a hospital tower just outside Newark. I had just turned fifty-six. She told me to be still. I asked her if it would hurt at all. She said no. She said I wouldn't feel a thing.

I lay there in a paper gown, counting backward from ten. I kept my eyes shut tight, but my mind was in a panic. It all started coming back up. The past. Weighing on my conscience like a violent debt. One I was about to repay. The nurse pushed a red button, and I disappeared into the tube.

I spent two days waiting on the results. The doctor called the house while my wife was at the store. We drove together to the clinic at noon the next day. I sat across from the doctor in a windowless room. His desk was a mess of paperwork and medical books. He placed a black-and-white MRI in front of me and said three little letters that slugged me in the sternum: A—L—S.

"Lou Gehrig's . . ." I said. He nodded to confirm my worst fears.

Time seemed to slow down as he explained my doomed future. His words came out warped, like a record spun in reverse. Like a distant radio signal. I didn't have the money to get sick. I imagined myself, helpless in a wheelchair. Unable to move. I was afraid I'd get dementia and forget my wife's name. I was afraid I'd forget the names of my children.

"How long do I have? To live?"

"It's hard to say," he said. "The disease affects everyone differently. I've had clients live ten, fifteen years. Others . . . months."

I left the hospital with my wife. Stared out the window. It was mid-December. I didn't feel like talking. Minutes passed slow. I could feel my body collapsing. This was it. I had escaped death before. Too many times to count. But it found me in the sub-urbs as a married man. And not in the way I thought it would. Not a bullet to the head, or a knife in the back. ALS was an invisible killer. Patient and methodical. That scared me more than twenty guys with machetes.

Finally, I spoke.

"How am I gonna tell the boys?"

"We'll do it together," she said. "I'll be right there the whole time. Beside you."

"I thought I paid my debt," I said.

"What debt?"

"To God. I thought we were square. That it was over. But here He is. Back again. To collect."

"It isn't your fault that you're sick, Aiden."

"You know the worst part? I know I deserve this. For what I did."

She pulled the car over to the shoulder and clicked on her hazards. She grabbed my cold hand and held it in hers. Cars sped by us as we idled on the side of the freeway.

"You were a kid, Aiden. Why are you so quick to blame yourself?"

———

White stadium floodlights blinded the field. We were down by three. Huddled mid-field with our helmets knocked together. I bit down on my mouthguard. Lungs were gassed. I could barely see through the sweat in my eyes.

It was 1982. I was sixteen years old. A junior in high school in a Jersey town we affectionately called the Bluffs.

The Bluffs was a small section of Jersey that seemed to exist in its own orbit. It had the buzz of city street life, but felt, at the same time, like a small town where every-body knew everybody. Nosy neighbors knew your business. People gossiped. Drive through on a weekday, and it might seem like a quiet slice of Americana. But beneath that facade pulsed a vicious, corrupted heart. The Bluffs was run by mobsters and street gangs. Heroin flowed in and out of the ports. There were more illegal guns on the street than cars. It was a breeding ground for criminals.

We'd done the play a thousand times. Fake left. Cut hard right. A short pass over the middle. First down.

"Aiden, you got this?"

I nodded. I was a wide receiver. The fate of the game rested on my shoulders. We took our positions. From the corner of my eye, I saw the high school cheerleaders. Their red-and-white pom-poms. Coach pacing at the ten. Next to him, my mother. I never saw my father at a game. He was too busy working at the transnational train company. But far off to the left, standing by himself, I saw another man: Eddy Tocino, dressed in black. Arms folded. His salt-and-pepper hair slicked back and to the side. Everybody knew who he was. Nobody dared to say it out loud.

Twelve seconds left in the half. The center snapped the ball.

I faked left. Broke right. The quarterback dropped back and threw a ten-yard bullet. I turned just in time to see the blur of brown leather spiraling toward me. The ball thudded into my sternum and stuck. I cradled it in my arms, turned, and collided with a linebacker who tackled me down into the turf at the seven-yard line.

It was a jarring hit. Like a car crash, it rag-dolled my head and neck. I was dazed under the lights. The whiplash dizzied me, and the taste of warm blood flooded my mouth from my bitten tongue.

This is what I lived for.

Violence is a drug. A rush of pure dope to the brain. A hit of serotonin like nothing I'd ever experienced. I got high off hitting someone as hard as I could. I got even higher when they'd hit me back.

I could feel my heartbeat pulsing in my temple. I saw spots and white stars under the cold black sky. Night games were rare in the Bluffs. The street gang turf wars made it too dangerous for us to play ball after dark. The Latin Kings and the Vice Lords had been lighting each other up. Some decades-old beef about drug corners and bragging rights. We'd see their cars rolling by with the headlights off, stalking their rivals, gunning each other down like we were at war. But here we were. Playing ball in the dark.

A voice slowly broke through the daze.

"Aiden, you okay? Get up!"

I felt like a soldier on a battlefield. And our team was like an infantry, gaining ground on the enemy, fighting together, pushing back, so close to occupying their turf. It was a war.

Two plays later, we scored the game's winning touchdown. I'd had one of the best games of my life. Received for 194 yards and three touchdowns. If my father had been there, he would've been proud of me that night.

I'm almost certain of that.

After I'd showered and changed, I walked the cinder-block tunnel from the locker room to the field. I saw Eddy, by himself, waiting by the concession stand. Eddy was a lieutenant in the DeCavalcante crime family. He was one of the most dangerous men in New Jersey. He was a friend of mine.

At sixteen, I wore two faces. One of a high school kid with all the promise of going all-state. The other of a young Mafia recruit. I'd put on one face each morning and ride my bike to school. Then after practice, I'd swap it for the other.

"You played a helluva game tonight," he said. His approval meant more to me than my own coach. More than my father. More than God. We walked together to his silver Mercedes parked in the back lot. "Heard there was a scout in the stands tonight."

"No shit?"

"Some recruiters from Michigan State."

"You talk to them?"

The dream was always to go to Nebraska or Ohio or Michigan to play college ball.

"You think I'm gonna lean on some college scout for you? Besides, you don't need anybody's help."

I threw my backpack on the floor and rode shotgun to the suburbs. We took the back roads slow. Drove across the city to a wealthy suburb just outside the city.

"You just missed the turn."

"I need you to do something for me first," he said.

"Tonight?"

"That a problem?"

I shook my head. No sir.

The job was simple. Jack a BMW from outside a house party two towns over. Bring it to the shop so Eddy and his crew could strip it for parts. I'd been running this game with Eddy since my sophomore year. He dropped me out near a small affluent suburb where the rich kids lived.

"In and out," he said. "Fast."

Then he sped off, leaving me alone on a dark street, holding my bag. I was a junior in high school. I could steal a car in less than sixty seconds, quicker than most guys twice my age.

You'd find some of the most idyllic suburbs in the state thirty minutes outside the Bluffs. Our racket was to sneak into wealthy suburbs and jack expensive cars. I quickly found a quiet street lined with luxury cars. I kept a low profile as I loitered for a while outside a stone Tudor mansion. The residential block was quiet. Some of the families had already begun decorating for Christmas. At the end of the street, I saw a new red BMW convertible. I unzipped my backpack and dug past my Algebra II book, my Spanish folder, my copy of *David Copperfield* and the Cliffs Notes I bought with it. I pulled out a screwdriver and a long metal slim jim. I was a sly little thief. I had done this six times before. I remembered every car I stole. Each time I did, I was faster than the time before.

I took one more glance around to make sure nobody was coming. Then I began: shimmied the metal rod down into the car door until I felt the lock. I shifted just slightly and heard a pop. Just like that, the door opened.

I tossed my backpack on the console and ducked inside. Adjusted the seat to fit my six-two frame and jammed the screwdriver into the ignition to start it. But something was off. The car wouldn't start.

"Fuck."

I searched through my backpack for a flashlight. If I was going to wire it to start, I'd need to be able to get under the steering wheel. And then I heard a voice from across the street.

"Hey, what the fuck are you doing?"

I stepped out of the car. "Go back inside before you get hurt," I said.

"Fuck you, buddy," he said, walking closer. "I'm callin' the cops."

But before that last word could even leave his mouth, I swung. My cold fist smacked with a hollow thud against his jaw. I slugged him twice in the stomach. He went down hard. I got on top of him and bashed his head against the street. Stood over him and struck hard with a swift knee to the ribs that left him gasping in the middle of the road.

"You call the cops, and I swear to God, I'll kill you."

I stood over him, looking down, this stranger, writhing and whimpering in pain and fear. And I noticed, even then, in the moment, how odd it was that I didn't feel anything. Not empathy, not sadness. Not even fear. I was eerily calm. Or maybe I was numb. I felt that something was missing inside of me. I had a junkie's appetite for violence.

With the guy still on the ground, I ducked back into the BMW. Now I was facing a possible assault charge on top of a grand theft charge. I needed to get out of there. I twisted on the flashlight. Reached under the wheel. Tugged on the tangle of wires. Touched the frayed ends together until I heard a spark. The dash lit up and the engine revved. Here we go. I adjusted the seat and closed the door. I heard police sirens in the distance. Some friendly neighbor must've called the police. I put the gear in drive and sped off.

I floored it through the quiet residential streets and onto the main street. Tires spun and squealed as I hooked right and saw cop lights in the rearview. I sped up. I felt like I was back on the football field. Hauling ass, gaining yards, with someone behind me, close enough to feel their breath on my neck. And me, running for my life.

But the cops didn't know the neighborhood like I did.

I jumped on the freeway and floored it west. Pulled off on the next exit. Hooked a U. Down a side street. Pulled into a high school. Sped through the parking lot and down an alley. I shut off the lights and waited. I jumped out of the car, adjusted the seat so it would look like a much smaller man was driving, and walked to the back of the alley.

Adrenaline rushed through my veins while I waited. I heard the sirens fade away. When it felt safe to leave, I jumped back into the car and drove the speed limit across town to the auto body shop.

I pulled the BMW into an open lane, where I saw Eddy waiting with a smile.

That night, I got home around eleven. Our two-story redbrick rowhouse sat on the corner of Leland and Sutherland Street. The windows were dark. The house was asleep. As usual, my mother left a key under the doormat. I let myself in. I tiptoed through the house. The floorboards creaked with every step. My father wasn't home. He never was. But my mother was a light sleeper. I tried never to disturb her.

I flipped the kitchen light. Scoured the fridge. Near the back, I saw some leftovers wrapped in tinfoil. I took the food out of the fridge and jumped back, startled. My mother was standing in the living room, holding a shoebox.

"Jesus Christ, you scared me."

"You wanna tell me where the hell this came from?"

My mother's native language was Hungarian. She met my father in Budapest and came with him to America in 1956, left during the Hungarian revolution. English was her second language and she spoke it in a broken, stilted cadence. She looked and sounded like Zsa Zsa Gabor, always impeccably dressed and made up. I inherited so much of my personality from my mother. She was quick tempered. She never held back. She carried herself with a fearlessness I would later carry myself.

She opened the shoebox and took out a rubber-banded wad of hundreds.

"I counted eleven thousand dollars," she said. "That sound right to you?"

"Mom . . ."

"Don't lie to me, Aiden. I wanna know what you're up to. Where the hell does a sixteen -year-old get eleven thousand dollars? In cash?"

"Do you really wanna know?"

"Aiden, you know what your father will say if he finds out you're hanging out with those guys. You got your whole life ahead of you."

"What are you worried about?"

"Just promise me you're being careful. I worry about you."

"I promise, Mom."

I searched my mother's face to see a glimmer of her true feelings, but I only found her shyness. She hated confrontation. She didn't want the truth. She thought she was protecting me by loving me unconditionally. I let her believe that.

I took the shoebox full of money from her and kissed her on the cheek.

"It's late," I said. "I got school in the morning."

For my mother, it was all about appearances.

She was born Eva Varga. Grew up in a sleepy, tree-lined district of Buda, Hungary, just north of the Danube River. She lived in Hungary during World War II, falling asleep every night as Allied bombers decimated her city. My father was from south of the river, the slums of Pest. They met as teenagers and married shortly after. They never spoke about their lives in Budapest. Their eyes harbored secrets. I didn't know at the time that understanding their secrets from Hungary would end up being the key to unlocking my own.

I adored my mother. I was an unashamed, self-proclaimed mama's boy. She learned I was dyslexic when I was six years old. She never told me. Having a dyslexic kid brought too much shame to the family. What would people think if they knew I couldn't read?

Outside of football, I hated school. I didn't belong in a classroom. I wasn't like the other kids. The inner workings of my mind were pure chaos. I could barely read. Words danced on the page. Numbers appeared in reverse order. Nothing stood still. Nothing made sense. I was always falling behind and didn't know why. Football was my only shot at getting into college.

———————

The Saturday after I jacked the BMW, I was making collections from the corners Eddy owned, my backpack stacked with envelopes full of money from gambling debts.

I wasn't book smart, but I had a criminal's mind. I was moving up the ranks in Eddy's crew, fast. But too many guys still saw me as a kid. I was Eddy's boy. I'd been running errands for the crew since I was twelve. I knew I'd never be anything more than a small-time car thief unless I did something to change their perceptions of me.

I rode my bike ten miles until I reached the shop two towns over. Inside it was dark, but I could hear a man screaming. I saw a yellow sliver of light from under a door that led to the toolshed. I opened the door and saw Eddy and six guys from our crew standing in a semicircle around a man beaten bloody in a heap.

"Oh, hey Aiden," Eddy said. He was nonchalant. Unaffected by the man bleeding on his shoes.

"Who's he?"

"Oh, him? He's just a guy who thought he could fuck me," Eddy said, and he kicked him in the ribs. The guy let out a pathetic yelp. "He's a cocksucker who owes me money but thinks he can make a fool outta me."

"No, Eddy . . ." the guy begged. "Please . . . I have two little girls. Please don't kill me."

"Kill you?" Eddy said. Then he turned to me. "What do you think, Aiden? Should we kill him?"

I shook my head no. "He's no good to you dead," I said. Inside, I knew this was a test. It was my chance to erase the perception of the crew that I was a kid. I needed to do something they would never forget. Something that made it clear that I was every bit as ruthless as Eddy.

"Don't kill him," I said. "Death is too easy. Pick him up."

Out of the corner of my eye, I saw a rusted metal bench vise. I didn't even know his name. I didn't care. I slugged him twice in the stomach and he keeled over. I opened the vise, grabbed the guy by the ears, and dragged him to the table and jammed his head in the vise.

"Whoa, whoa, whoa," Eddy said. "You don't gotta do this, Aiden."

But I'd become unhinged. The crew took a step back. Not even Eddy could stop me. I wasn't just trying to kill this man—I was killing whatever was left of the little kid inside of me.

His head was shoved sideways in the vise. I began to twist the crank. As the metal enclosed on his face, I heard his muffled yelps for help. I heard his nose bone crack and I kept cranking until I couldn't turn it any further. His arms went limp at his sides. Eddy rushed over and pulled me off. Uncranked the vise and pulled his head from the metal. The guy collapsed in a heap onto the oil-slicked floor. Eddy checked his pulse.

"He's breathing," he said. "Let's get him the fuck out of here."

As I stood there, watching them drag this man away, I didn't feel anything. Looking back now, I wonder: When did I become that person? Was it a form of self-preservation? Did I have to be numb to survive in this world? Or was it something else?

After that night, the crew never saw me as a kid again. I became Eddy's personal enforcer.

The new role kept me busy. Being an enforcer was a job that required me to do a bit of everything for Eddy. Sometimes I acted as his driver. Other times, we ran errands together. I made collections for him on gambling debts. But my main focus was to protect him at any cost. I was something like a bodyguard and his own personal pit bull. Violence was always a last resort, but there was always somebody, somewhere who thought they could stiff Eddy and not pay up. That's when I'd pay them a visit with a baseball bat or an ice pick.

Eddy and I grew closer. He took me under his wing and schooled me on the business. I drove him to meetings and waited in the car. After a few months—by then I was seventeen—he started inviting me in. I'd sit quietly beside him and soak up whatever I could. I struggled in the classroom but had a savant's mind for organized crime. I was good at it.

Couple months later. Summer in the Bluffs. Humid, sticky heat. Neighborhood kids skipped rope and splashed in the puddles of busted street hydrants. School was out for the summer and I was spending less time with my friends and more time with Eddy and the crew. It never felt unusual for me to be surrounded by older men. I never got along with kids my own age and, unconsciously, was likely seeking a father figure with my father being gone so often.

Lunch that day was at the Three Brothers Diner—a small, mom-and-pop haunt on a derelict corner in the Bluffs. It wasn't much to look at—half a dozen worn leather booths and a counter where you could grab a quick coffee or a plate of eggs. It reeked of ham grease and burnt hash browns. But they made the best corned beef sandwich on the East Coast. Homemade pickles. Just the right amount of mustard.

We were regulars. The place was something like a second office to Eddy and his crew. It's where we'd all gather to hang, talk shop, shoot the shit. The waitresses loved us. The owners treated us like family. There was always a table waiting when he came in, which was almost every day. Eddy always tipped big—he believed in taking care of locals that made the Bluffs feel like a neighborhood. Whatever else he was—a criminal, a con man—he cared about the Bluffs.

As usual, we took the back booth—just the three of us, Eddy, Dominik, and me. Dominik was Eddy's right-hand man. His number two in command. His lieutenant. Dominik advised on major projects and took a lead role on a lot of the operations. He was morbidly obese—closing in on three hundred pounds—with a belly that hung over his belt. He was known as a hothead, and even at seventeen, I saw that blank, sociopath stare. From the first time I met Dominik, he never seemed to like me. Maybe it was because I was "Eddy's boy." Maybe he felt threatened, that Eddy was grooming somebody else to be his second-in-command. Of course, my lack of Italian heritage would've prevented me from climbing to the heights I wanted within the crew, but still, something about my mere existence seemed to rub Dominik the wrong way.

Eddy and Dominik had been running together since they were my age—seventeen years old. They were close as brothers, or at least there was a time when they were. At that time, it seemed something was coming between them. Some unspoken animosity. Call it jealousy or resentment. Maybe Dominik didn't want to be number two his whole life. I was too young to know. Whatever it was I could sense it, boiling under the surface.

There was no air-conditioning inside the Three Brothers deli. Just a small box fan that blew hot, recycled air through the claustrophobic space. It was sweltering as we ordered our food. Eddy and Dominik both ordered pasta fagioli. I ordered a sandwich—corned beef on rye with mustard and pickles. Halfway through the lunch, Eddy spots a guy out the diner window walking westward down the block.

"See that wop fuck right there," Eddy says. "Cocksucker owes me twelve grand."

"Who?" I said. "That piece of shit right there?"

"Yeah."

"Who is he?"

"Louis Gatz."

"Gatz? Doesn't he own that billiards parlor across from the firehouse?"

"That's him."

"Well, how come he's still walking?"

"What am I gonna do? He keeps telling me he's gonna get the scratch, and then I never hear from him."

It wasn't like Eddy to be passive. He'd usually take a hard-line, aggressive approach to a guy who owed him that kind of money. I'd seen him break people's kneecaps for a lot less. So why was he being so calm about it all? At seventeen—hungry for attention and validation—I interpreted his defeatist response as a challenge. Eddy knew I had a killer instinct. In a way, I thought he was testing me.

So with my sandwich still in my hand, I pushed my chair out and went hauling ass out of the diner and across the street. I could hear them calling after me to stop, but I was like a rabid pit bull. I couldn't be reasoned with. I ran up beside Gatz, sandwich in hand. He must've heard my heavy footsteps stomping behind him, because he turned in a scared panic.

"You Louis?" I asked.

"Who wants to know?"

I never answered. Instead, I swung so hard, my fist like a sledgehammer, and almost punched through his jaw. He collapsed in a heap. I slit him up with kicks to the ribs. Right hooks to the kidneys. He was begging me to stop. I stomped on his wrist and heard him scream out in pain. As I laid a biblical beating down on this degenerate gambler, I could feel Eddy and Dominik run up behind me. Eddy stood to the side of me, watching, while Dominik got a few shots in of his own.

I reared back and swiftly kicked the guy in the ribs and heard the air get knocked out of him. All the while, I was still holding onto my sandwich. I took a bite.

"This fuckin' kid's eating a sandwich," Dominik said. He had a bemused grin on his face. "He just fucked this guy up with one hand, while eating a corned beef sandwich. Hey 'Sandwich,' let's get outta here before the cops come."

After that day, Louis Gatz paid Eddy the twelve g's he owed him. And the nickname "Sandwich" stuck for life. To the guys in the crew, I was no longer Aiden—I was Sandwich.

———————

Later, back at the garage, something had come over Dominik. I could tell something was nagging at him, and it simmered inside, slowly rising to a boil; he started up with me about not following orders. At that point, despite being Eddy's enforcer, Dominik saw me as an understudy. An intern. A kid who should only act when given an order. To him, I was some measly frontline soldier. An infantryman. When he saw me take matters into my own hands—jumping up from the table like I did—it spooked him. He didn't like that I went rogue, defying him like that, especially in front of Eddy. I could tell he felt emasculated. Truth was, he was threatened by a seventeen-year-old taking his spot and he thought he could bully me into obedience.

"Didn't you hear me calling after you? Telling you to slow down?"

"No."

"No? You fuckin' deaf or what? You don't go tuning some guy up in broad daylight. You're begging the cops to seize this place. That ain't how we do shit."

"It needed to be done."

"That's not your call to make. Or I need to remind you who you work for?"

"I work for Eddy, not you."

"You work for the crew. And I'm a lieutenant of this crew and you're gonna give me some respect."

"Fuck off."

"What'd you say?"

But before I could answer, he slugged me twice in the stomach, sending me down to a knee. It felt like I'd been sacked on the twenty-yard line. His second punch knocked the wind out of me. Rage boiled inside of me. Rushed through my body to my face where I could feel a vein pulsing in my forehead.

"What the fuck you doin'?" Eddy said. "Leave the kid alone. He's one of us."

"He ain't one of us," Dominik said. But before he could say another word, I reached behind me and picked up a lead pipe slick with oil and swung it wildly, blasting Dominik in the sternum. I hauled back and swung again, this time crushing his shoulder, and again, connecting with the point of his elbow. He crumpled onto the floor. But he was quickly back up.

"Knock it the fuck off, the both of you," Eddy yelled. "I'm the captain of this crew. You do what I say. Now knock it off."

Dominik's nostrils were flaring. He had murder swelling in his eyes.

"You little prick. I oughta kill you for that."

"I said shut up!" Eddy yelled. "We're a family. Now shake hands and grow the fuck up. It's over. There ain't gonna be a civil war here."

After a moment of cooldown, both Dominik and I relented and agreed to follow orders like the soldiers we were. My job was to protect Eddy. Period. I dropped the pipe. It made a loud, metallic echo on the concrete floor. And I reached out to shake Dominik's hand.

As the summer waned on, the jobs got more and more dangerous. One weekend, Eddy asked me to make a collection for him. Some degenerate gambler—Wyatt Something—was refusing to pay up, and he needed me to pay him a visit. Give him a warning. Wyatt Something worked at a massage parlor. One of those off-the-books, strip mall joints. I went around back where I knew he took his smoke breaks and waited for him. In those days, I never carried a gun, but I had my ice pick hidden up the sleeve of my windbreaker. After about twenty minutes, Wyatt Something came out. His face dropped when he saw me.

"Eddy's been looking for you," I said.

He looked around, wild-eyed, like a scared and cornered animal.

"The fuck are you?"

"Never mind all that. You been bullshittin' him long enough. I'm gonna need to see some money today, or you start paying points."

He squinted at me. I could tell from the way his skin looked, from the pale color of his eyes, that he was a druggie. The money he owed us was long gone. Probably snorted up his nose or shot into his arm. Eddy shouldn't have ever allowed this guy to gamble with us when he knew he wasn't good for it. It was a greedy, shortsighted mistake and now things were about to turn violent.

"Man, why don't you go fuck yourself," he shouted, hocking a snotty wad of spit in my direction. Before his spit hit the asphalt, my ice pick was sliding down my jacket sleeve and into my palm. But he beat me to the punch. He had a small blade of his own drawn and jabbed me in the side with it, ripping a gash in my abdomen.

I screamed out in pain and went down. He bolted inside and locked the door. The gash was bad, bleeding out into my palm and soaking through my T-shirt. I pressed my hand into the wound, but it only caused the gushing to worsen. I needed to get to a hospital, but a hospital stay would invite the cops, and I couldn't have that. So I limped back to my car, hopped inside, and floored it back to the garage, where Eddy was waiting for me. He was on the phone when I went hobbling into the office.

"Jesus Christ," he said. "Dom, lemme call you back." He slammed the phone down. "The fuck happened to you."

"Cocksucker knifed me," I said.

"He got you pretty good," Eddy said.

"I'm gonna bleed to death," I said. I was starting to feel light-headed. I could feel my heart thudding in my chest, and blood pumped out of the wound at pace with my heart rate.

"Call Doctor Yelavarthi," Eddy called out to one of the other guys in the room. "Tell him it's an emergency."

Less than twenty minutes later, a small Indian man of about fifty showed up. He was mild-mannered. He had almost no reaction when he saw me drenched in blood. Yelavarthi stayed calm and he inspected the gushing wound. He was a surgeon in Vietnam, and I knew he'd seen much worse in the Hanoi field hospitals. He sopped up the blood with a white towel. Applied a stinging disinfectant that burned so badly I nearly lost consciousness. Pain went quivering through my body. Eddy handed me a shot of Crown Royal. Anything to take the edge off the pain. And then, I felt a cold needle puncture my skin, and the strange, dragging sensation of sutures being threaded through my skin. He patched me up that night and saved my life. I never went to the hospital. The cops never heard a peep about the incident.

It always amazed me how far the Mafia's reach could go. It didn't stop at cops and politicians. It reached doctors, too. Back then, we had our own underground community.

I couldn't tell anybody what I was involved with. Not my parents, not even my closest friends. Over the years, there were three people who saved my life, all at different times, and in very different ways. Dr. Yelavarthi was one of them. The other two were neighborhood kids I'd known since junior high: Sam Schwartz and Donnie Cooper.

I first met Sam in the seventh grade. I could never forget the first time I saw him, standing there on the side of the basketball court, waiting quietly to be chosen for a team. He was five-four with braces, and he weighed less than a hundred pounds, with feet so big that they looked like clown shoes. The poor kid had no coordination. I watched him that day, struggling not to trip over his laces. But what he lacked in coordination, he made up for in smarts. He was painfully shy but remarkably intelligent. A math whiz like nothing I had ever seen before. I could never overemphasize just how geeky this kid was. He knew math the way I knew crime. Our minds were wired differently, but there was something—some unknowable thing—that drew us toward each other. Maybe it was feeling like an outcast. Sam was a gawky, Jewish kid in a part of town that didn't always respect his culture. I knew what that was like— feeling left out, unwanted. Neither of us felt like we belonged. No group wanted us, so we started our own.

Not too long after, I met Donnie Cooper. Another kid from the Bluffs, Donnie and I played football together. He wasn't the sharpest tool in the shed, but the kid had heart. He lived just a couple houses down and we'd hang together every day—riding bikes, wandering the streets, complaining about teachers, girls, and our coaches' latest antics. Donnie was loyal as a dog, and I knew he had my back. Back then, I could never have imagined Sam, Donnie, and I would be building a friendship that would last over four decades. We were just lost boys who found each other.

But no matter how much of our lives we shared, I could never tell them about my secret life with Eddy and the mob. Even to my two closest friends in the world, I lied. I would tell them I was caddying at the local golf club, then I'd slip off and meet Eddy at the garage. Why did I lie? Because I didn't think they'd understand. I wasn't sure I understood myself. Sam had smarts, and Donnie had sports. They both had a future. I wasn't sure I had anything outside of being a gangster. It was my ticket out—a ticket I wasn't sure they'd approve of. So I kept it to myself.

As the months went by, Eddy started trusting me with bigger and bigger jobs. I began collecting the gambling debts guys owed. Began sitting in on important meetings. I was moving up the ladder. I knew if f I didn't make it playing football, I could make a decent life for myself with Eddy.

On a Tuesday in September of my senior year, I rode my bike two miles across town to meet up with Eddy and the crew at the auto body shop. The guys were playing cards. Watching golf on an old Magnavox. The plan that day was to go down to a quiet, suburban block and jack a BMW. But then Eddy walked into the room with a concerned look on his face. He turned the TV off. Told us to put the cards down. We had to talk.

He pulled a chair out and sat at the head of the table.

"Listen," he said, and he took a big deep breath. "I just got word from my guy over in county. The feds are looking to hit us. I don't know when. But he says it could be soon as this weekend."

"For fuck's sake," Paulie said. "Somebody talking?"

Paulie shot me a look. "Don't look at me, motherfucker. I've been here since I was twelve years old and I've never said a goddamn word to anybody."

"You ain't one of us," he said. "That's all I'm gonna say."

He was right.

As much as I hated to admit it, there was a truth I'd been running from: I wasn't Italian. I was Hungarian. And no matter many times Eddy told me I was part of the family, my heritage said otherwise. Only Italians got made. And being a made guy meant you were untouchable. It meant more money. It meant you called your own shots and had a crew of you own. It was what every wiseguy dreamed of. But for me, it wasn't possible. No matter what I did, I'd always be an outsider looking in.

"Sit down," Eddy said. "I'm not gonna let this bullshit cause a rift. Leave Aiden the fuck outta this. We ain't done shit wrong."

"You're always protecting him? The fuck's he got on you?"

"I said shut your mouth!" Eddy yelled. "We're a family, capiche? This shit goes down and the subpoenas start flying, it hurts all of us. So, for the time being, we all need to split up."

A voice came from the back. "Split up?" Little Johnny.

"Just until things cool down," Eddy said.

"And what if they don't?" I asked.

Eddy drags his hands over his face. "Look. You watch the news? You saw what happened in Providence. In New York."

What had happened was, the Department of Justice had been nabbing DeCavalcante crew members left and right. Crews were going down, getting locked up. Major RICO trails were pending. The heat was cranked as high as it could go for guys like us. "We got fuckin' rats on our ship and we have to get to shore before the goddamn boat sinks. Okay?"

"Where the fuck you want us to go?" Paulie asked.

"Anywhere. Just get out of here. For a while. It isn't safe for us anymore."

The truth was, I always knew it would end this way. Ninety percent of these guys end up dead or in jail. That was a reality I couldn't get away from. And I felt a twinge of sadness and guilt for some of the guys who'd given their lives to the crew. Because I had football. I had a way out.

The garage was slowly emptying out, one guy at a time, when I heard Eddy call my name.

"Aiden," he said. "Hang back for a sec. I need to talk to you. How you doin' with all this shit? You okay?"

"I dunno. It's gonna be hard not seeing you around."

"It's not goodbye forever," he said, and my eyes redirected to the concrete floor.

"Hey, what did I say about looking down like that. Look me in the eye. It's not goodbye forever, okay?"

I nodded.

"Listen. You know I've always considered you like a son. I wanna be straight up with you. There's a good chance I'm not gonna make it outta this."

"What do you mean?"

"My lawyer says there's a ninety percent chance I get indicted in all this. I gotta disappear, kiddo."

"Disappear? Where?"

"I'm leaving for Spain," he said. "End of the week."

"Spain?"

"My old lady's got a cousin there. Gonna drink some wine and flamenco until things cool down around here. Sounds pretty good, yeah?"

"You got room for me?" I said and smiled sadly. I was an only child, and this crew was the closest thing I ever had to a brotherhood.

"Nah," he says. "You need to go to school, Aiden. You need to play football. These other guys . . . this life is all they know. But you got a gift. You need to promise me you won't squander it."

The football season came to end. We didn't take state, but we finished with a winning record. At the same time, the crew had all but disbanded. The auto body shop closed. And my heart and mind were torn. I felt a sort of freedom—a relief—at being released from the crew. I wanted to play football and I saw only trouble ahead if I kept running jobs for Eddy. How long before I ended up in jail, or worse? The Mafia had a way of devouring your time. Your life. They wanted ownership over your body and your soul. I wasn't ready to give it to them. I had a separate dream that was supposed to rescue me from the streets. In March, I accepted a full-ride offer to Michigan State.

But my decision was complicated, and the feelings that came with it weren't always so clear-cut. I was an only child. I was a lonely kid. I wasn't a good student, and I didn't fit in anywhere. Even my football teammates felt distant to me. I couldn't make a connection. But with Eddy and the guys, it was different. They were criminals, yes. But they got me in a way nobody else ever had. They watched out for me. Mentored me. They made me feel like I mattered.

I was going to miss that.

I graduated from high school in May of 1984. Summer passed in a blur. By late August, it was time to say goodbye to my little section of Jersey. I packed up my room, loaded up the car, and drove with my parents for two days across country to East Lansing, Michigan. Apparently shipping me off for a discount was something my father could show up for.

When we finally arrived on campus, my father parked his black Caddy outside of Kentwood Hall—a two-story redbrick residence that reminded me of home. We lugged the boxes up the stairs to the second floor while Mom took my duffel bag up in the elevator. My room was the last door on the right. I claimed the top bunk. Dad helped me tack my torn Tampa Bay Buccaneers poster to the wall. Even though I grew up in Jersey, I loved the Buccaneers and dreamed of signing a big contract with Tampa and buying a big house on the Florida coast.

My father patted me on the back. I wanted to grab him and hug him before he walked out, but we didn't have the kind of relationship. Instead, I just nodded and waved goodbye. Kissed my mother on the cheek and wished them a safe ride home. And when they left, the quiet in the dorm room was too much to bear. Who was I without Eddy? Who was I without the crew backing me up? I chose the straight life, but now I wasn't so sure.

———————

College was a bust from the get-go. No matter hard I fought it, I felt homesick. I felt like a stranger on campus. Displaced and invisible, small and unseen. I missed having the respect that came from running with Eddy and the guys. In the Bluffs, people knew me. People feared me. But here? I was just another student on campus, and I hated standing in line and waiting my turn.

Saturday mornings were for running drills. Practice started at seven, when it was still dark. We ran the bleachers. Then it was short, explosive sprints around the track. I tried to make friends with the other guys on the team, but it didn't take. I thought about joining a frat to have some sort of brotherhood, but I couldn't fit in. I kept to myself. I took some business courses and sat in the back. I ate by myself in the cafeteria. I missed the guys. I missed my city. I missed my mother's cooking.

After the blues of the first month wore off, I rededicated myself to football. I slept with a football by my bed as if it were an affirmation. I touched the Buccaneers poster like it were a prayer card. I had to make the most of my time here. I swore an oath to myself that I would make it to the big leagues.

Then, on a warm day in late August , I was walking back to my dorm after practice. There was a calm in the air I never experienced back in Jersey. Inside the residence hall, freshmen played Ping-Pong and bullshitted in the lounge. Down the hall, the doors were chaotic messes of sticky notes and Pink Floyd posters and "Vote for Mondale" stickers. I had my backpack slung on my shoulder and burst into my dorm room. And I froze.

I saw a man in a gray suit sitting at my desk. I'd never seen him before. Standing beside him was another man in a blue suit. I could tell they weren't here to kill me or collect a debt. I glanced for just a second at the Buccaneers poster on the wall. My heart plummeted into my guts and my mouth went dry. I stood there still and scared in the doorway until one of them spoke.

"Aiden Gabor?"

"Who the fuck are you two?"

"I'm Agent Johnson," he said and flashed me his badge. "Department of Justice. Let's go for a ride."

CHAPTER 2

R iding I-75 in the back of an unmarked. Two feds in the front and me in the back. Gunning it west toward Detroit. Going ninety, no siren. Nobody said a word.

I sat in the back, behind a pane of bulletproof glass, hands clenched, knee shaking. Worry clouded my mind. I didn't know where they were taking me. I wasn't sure if I'd ever play football again. Or taste my mother's cooking.

With East Lansing in the rearview, I got up the nerve to speak. I cleared my throat and leaned against the glass. "You gonna tell me where you're taking me or what?"

"Nowhere special," one of the agents said, turning in his seat so he could see me better. "Just a quiet place so we can talk."

"Talk about what?" I asked. "I got nothing to say." But the agent riding shotgun just smiled. "Just enjoy the ride," he said.

The traffic was gridlocked going the other way. I sat quietly in the back of that silver '78 Dodge, watching the city turn to farmland as we floored it out of East Lansing. Soon the freeway road narrowed and the double-yellow disappeared. And the whole ride I stared out the window and wondered: What did they know? What did they want from me? How far was I willing to go to protect Eddy?

The run to downtown Detroit took an hour-fifteen. We pulled fast off the main road and into the parking lot of a Howard Johnson's. I was disoriented and confused about why we were stopping here. Were there other agents inside? Was I going to be cuffed and arrested?

The taller of the two agents walked around the car and let me out. He was kind of gangly, with sharp dark eyes. He hiked his belt and adjusted his holster. He wanted me to know he was armed. The second agent walked beside me. He was sturdier than the other. Shorter and solidly built. As we walked together through the near-empty lot, my eyes darted around. Our car was one of four. There weren't too many people around. And I wondered—briefly—if I could make a break for it. But I quickly ruled against it. I was never the fastest on the football field, and I'd been nursing a banged-up ankle from a recent scrimmage. I didn't exactly trust my ankle to hold up in a high-stakes footrace.

Inside the restaurant, it was calm and dim and depressingly day quiet. The air smelled like stale Marlboros. The carpet was stained with old coffee spills and a lonely local sat at the counter, reading the paper, moving around scrambled eggs.

I followed the agents to a red vinyl booth tucked way off in the back. Some busboy wiped the table down with a wet rag and a waiter dropped off three glasses of sink water. I slid in. Kept my eyes fixed on a chipped glass ashtray while the agents casually paged through the laminated menu.

"Why don't we start with some formal introductions," the taller agent said. "I'm Agent Jackson. This is my partner, Agent Douglas."

"You gonna tell me what I'm doing here?"

Jackson smiled at Douglas and deflected the question. "You hungry, Aiden?" Then he smirked at Douglas. I could tell this was fun for them. They found some twisted amusement in the cruelty of dragging this out. "Go ahead," he said. "Get whatever you want. It's our treat."

Douglas chimed in. "Might be the last decent meal you have for a while."

I shook my head no.

My insides were twisted and riddled with panic. But I wasn't about to let them know it. I kept my jaw locked tight. If I showed fear, it was over.

Jackson lit up a menthol. Blew the smoke out the side of his mouth. He didn't say a word. He was tough to read, even for me. We just stared at each other. A standoff. A stalemate to see who would blink first. He smiled and took another drag. Ashed his cigarette in the glass tray and waved down the waitress. It was all part of his strategy. Tactical cop bullshit to lull me into a false sense of security.

"Hey, hon," Jackson said. Her name tag said Mabel. "Lemme get a short stack. Sausage. And are you brewing any decaf?"

She nodded.

"Let me get a cup. Two cream, two sugar."

"And for you, sweetie?" Mabel asked, glancing at me, smacking her lips as she chewed her gum.

"I'm fine."

Douglas handed her the menu with a gesture that indicated nothing for him. Then, with the ordering out of the way and the game playing over, Jackson kicked things off with a little small talk.

"We understand you're a hell of a ballplayer, Aiden." he said.

"Just cut the bullshit," I said. "What do you want?"

"C'mon, Aiden. You know why you're here."

"I don't know shit."

"No? You're just a normal kid, right?" he said, tossing a folder with my name scribbled in black pen on the table. "Let me ask you something, Aiden. Do you think you're sitting here right now because we *don't* know who you are?"

I stared at the folder and scrambled to get my lies straight. My hands began to shake. I willed them still. I took a deep breath and opened the folder and saw a xeroxed copy of my rap sheet. Below it: blown-up photographs. Grainy black-and-whites of Eddy and me outside the garage. At the diner. I thumbed through the photographs as my heart raced and then plummeted into my guts. It was as if they'd been watching me my whole life. There were a couple shots of Paulie—one of Eddy's top guys—and me. And some candid photos from the cookouts with the DeCavalcante crew.

My breathing raced as I paged through the photographs. My head was swimming. I swallowed hard a few times, then stammered out the only words I knew to say. Words I'd learned from the movies:

"I wanna talk to a lawyer."

"Sure," Jackson said calmly. "We can do that. You talk to a lawyer, and we can't protect you anymore."

"Protect me from what?"

As Jackson ran down my rap sheet, his voice slowed to a slur of warped distortion, like a record in reverse. His words echoed in my head and my knee started to shake.

"We're talking major crimes. Grand theft. Extortion. Racketeering. Embezzlement. Conspiracy to commit murder."

"Fuck that, I never killed nobody," I said.

But for the first time in a long time, I was scared. Shell-shocked. I nodded mutely and held my breath. I could feel my face run pale. The life drained from my eyes. Looked around the diner as the panic set in. There was a rumble of seasickness through my belly, and my mouth ran dry. And the only thing I could imagine was my mother's face. How could I tell her what I'd done? How was I supposed to tell her that my life was over?

"You could be looking at seventy years," Douglas said.

"You'll be almost ninety years old when you get out of prison," Jackson said. "That's your whole life."

If they were bluffing, I couldn't tell at the time. And I wish I could go back and tell the kid sitting in that booth to keep his mouth shut. They were just trying scare me. But at the time, I didn't know what kind of cards they were holding. And I could only keep up my tough-guy act for so long. They had me cornered. I felt myself starting to crumble. Still, I sat quietly. Fought off the panic. I was only eighteen. Could I spend the rest of my life in prison?

"We can arrest you right now. Right here. In front of all these people. Is that what you want, Aiden?"

I started to cave. "What do you want to know?"

Douglas looked at Jackson and laughed. They had me cornered and they knew it.

"Let's start from the beginning," Jackson said and pointed to the photographs. "How do you know these guys?"

"Friends," I said. "From the neighborhood."

"Friends?" he said with a bemused grin. He took a drag of his cigarette. "Some friends you got there. I'm curious how does a kid like you get mixed up with guys like this?"

"I don't know," I said. "However people meet people, I guess. They were guys my dad knew."

As soon as the words came out of my mouth, I knew I'd said too much.

"Your dad?" Douglas said, interrupting. "He wasn't around much, was he?"

I squinted at him across the table, and said, "Watch your fuckin' mouth about my father."

They were twisting the knife. Jackson's grin was antagonizing. Douglas was almost daring me to take a swing. They'd love nothing more than to have me face-down and cuffed on the carpet for assaulting an officer. His eyes said, C'mon. I know you want to. And I did. But all I could do was swallow it and stare back down at the table.

"I'm serious," he said. "Musta been hard growing up like that. Your daddy always gone. Lotta long trips to Vegas, right? While you're stuck at home. Taking care of

Mom. Lotta responsibility for a young kid. What's that saying? If Dad isn't home, the boy will find a father in the streets. Isn't that right? Is that what happened, Aiden?"

"I don't know."

"Did he know you were hanging out with Eddy Tocino?"

"No."

"No? Seems strange, doesn't it? If I was hanging around with a known felon, my parents would know about it. Tell me, where's Eddy now?"

"I'm not saying shit."

"No? Or maybe you don't know shit. Maybe you and Eddy weren't that close."

I smiled and shook off his lame attempts at reverse psychology. I kept mindlessly thumbing through the photos. Trying to come up with a way out of this.

"I did a little digging on you," Jackson said, interrupting. "Gotta say. Pretty impressive numbers you were putting up on the football field. But you weren't much of a student, were you? Didn't have many friends at school, did you, Aiden? Then you get mixed up with these mobsters, except you're not Italian. Never heard of an Italian mobster named Gabor. Where you from anyway? Don't tell me, I got it right here. Dad's from Budapest, right?"

"Hungarian," Douglas said, chiming in. "How does a Hungarian kid wind up as the enforcer for a guinea in the Bluffs?"

Jackson laughed and sipped his coffee. "Must be hard being part of a crew that doesn't want you. What'd you think was gonna happen?" he asked. "You know you gotta be Italian to get made. They were never gonna open the books for some Hungarian kid. So, what the fuck? What gives?"

"You're never gonna be one of them, Aiden," Douglas said. "It's sad to say but seems to me like you never belonged anywhere. They were just using you."

"I'd almost feel bad for you if you weren't such a fuckup," Jackson said. "You're a man without a country."

"Fuck off," I finally said.

The waitress broke the tension when she arrived with Jackson's breakfast. She set a steaming hot cup of decaf beside his plate. He twisted out his cigarette.

"Let's cut the bullshit, Aiden," he said. "You're knee deep in shit right now. Okay? And I promise, unless you start cooperating, this doesn't end well."

I swallowed hard but stayed stone-faced. I couldn't let them see the fear inside me.

"Now, we don't give a fuck about you," he said. "You're not the one we're after. But you're looking at some serious time behind bars for what you got yourself mixed up in."

"C'mon, Aiden."

"I swear on my mother."

"Your mother?" he said and nodded at Douglas, who slid a photograph of my mother across the table. It was her. It looked like it was taken while she was standing outside our house. She had no idea she was being targeted. And something about it felt like a robbery. Like they'd broken into our family life and stolen a moment that wasn't theirs.

"Why the fuck do you have that?"

He shot back with another question: "What did your mother know about all this?"

"My mother? You're gonna come after my mother? Leave my fuckin' mother out of this."

"That's not how it works, Aiden. Did your mom know you were jacking cars? Running illegal betting? She wasn't helping you, was she?"

"I said you leave her out of this."

Then Douglas slammed his fist down on the table. "Aiden!" he shouted. He was done playing around. "We got you beat. You understand. We own you."

Jackson intervened. Something about their banter felt rehearsed. Good cop bad cop shit. Jackson was playing the good guy. The cop I should trust. He was the one with compassionate eyes. He said, "Aiden, I don't wanna haul you outta here in cuffs. There is one other option."

The table fell silent, and I caught my breath. Quietly I said: "What's the other option?"

"You can work with us," he said. "Become an informant."

"An informant? You mean a rat?"

"No. You'll just be helping us collect some information on some really bad people."

"And if I agree?"

"Then we'll talk. See if we can reach a deal that keeps you out of jail."

We left the diner around two and they drove back to campus. I closed my eyes. Rested my forehead against the window. A part of me hoped I could fall asleep and wake up in a different reality. I never cried but I wanted to fall apart. I wanted to run home to my family and cry in the arms of my mother. The entire ride back to campus, I wondered how I was going to tell my family. What could I tell them? I stared out the window, watching Michigan pass by. The agents played the radio the whole ride back. I felt the weight of a looming life sentence crushing down on my chest.

Back in East Lansing, the agents dropped me on the curb outside my dorm.

"Think about our offer, Aiden. We'll be in touch."

Then they drove out of the parking lot, down the street, and out of sight. I had ten days to decide.

———————

That night, after the lights went out in Kentwood Hall, I sat on my bed, staring at the ceiling. I spun a football in my hands, as my mind raced and worried, rehashing the threat of a pending life sentence. If the agents were successful at anything, it was forcing me into a situation that reminded me of how alone I was. I couldn't ask my family for help. I couldn't ask my friends. I couldn't ask the crew. I couldn't ask my teammates. I was alone with this decision. It was mine to make.

I weighed my options. I could tell the agents to fuck off and take the sentence. Growing up, I was taught that's what men do. It's what Eddy and the guys would want me to do. Probably what my father would want, too. But it was easy for them to say when it wasn't their life on the line. I paced the hallways and imagined a life where I took the plea deal. Could I be a snitch? What would they want from me? Could I give up Eddy and the crew? I knew those guys. If they ever found out, they'd hunt me and kill me. They'd kill my entire family. I could die in prison at ninety, or I could die on the streets at eighteen. As I worked it out in my head, I figured I might be safer in jail than on the streets.

But there was a third option: I could run. Far away. Hide in some small town and change my name. Maybe they'd never find me.

I'd never play football.

The ten days that followed were a sleepless blur. I let the fear and worry gnaw away at me like termites tunneling through my insides, settling in my bones.

My whole world was collapsing around me. I stayed in my room and ate greasy takeout and slopped up ice cream. I got drunk on cheap beer and high on shitty corner dope. I was willing to do anything to escape, even for a minute, but nothing could distract me from the pending decision I had to make. At night, I'd walk alone through the campus, watching the other freshmen playing cards in the quad. Pulling all-nighters in the library stacks. They didn't know how lucky they were to have ordinary troubles. Whatever worries they had—grades and dating, finals and formals—seemed like small luxuries to me now. Even football, with all the pressure I'd put on myself to make it big, felt silly by comparison. I couldn't see it then. But now I had two roads to choose from. Both roads led to a different kind of hell: risk my life as an informer or die in jail.

I zoned out in the back of my business class. My professor droned on in front of a blackboard, but I couldn't focus. Nothing matters when the threat of prison is looming over your head. I stopped going to class. Stopped going out. Stopped showing up for football practice. I couldn't sleep. My dreams—when I had them—were nightmares of me running. Hiding in a closet where nobody could find me. I'd wake up in a panic and walk barefoot to the student lounge. I'd watch TV until I'd fall asleep on the couch.

My body was collapsing, too. A stress rash spread around both my armpits. A pimply stye jutted out from my right eye. I couldn't swallow. Couldn't blink. It felt like an ulcer was developing in my side and I was sure I was dying. My body was breaking down.

I know now what it really means to have a body that's failing. And it breaks my heart to think of myself then: young, healthy, my whole life ahead of me.

————————

The day before I was scheduled to meet back up with the agents, I took a bus out to the zoo. Bought an all-day pass and a large soda. I was leaning toward taking the sentence. I had my mother in my heart, telling me to work with the agents. But I had Eddy in my head. After all this time, he had control of my conscience. For better or worse, he was the man who set my moral compass.

I got to the zoo around noon. It was packed with out-of-towners. I wandered without a map, aimlessly going from section to section. I daydreamed about the way Eddy used to talk about the old-timers who'd do twenty years without saying a word. He spoke about them as if they were legends. Those were men. True tough guys from another era. Nowadays, everybody was a rat. But the DeCavalcante crew had a code, and I was part of that. And maybe I could do it. I could roll the dice with a lawyer and tough it out. With good behavior, maybe I'd be out before I was forty.

I ducked out of the sun and into the atrium where the African jungle snakes slithered around. I tapped on the glass. I spoke to the exotic birds, but they didn't talk back. Outside, I wandered past the giraffes, the flamingos, the chimpanzees who roughhoused while children watched on and parents took pictures.

Near the back of zoo, where they kept the pandas, I took a rest on the bench and watched them lumber around. Their faces looked so human. So expressive. And I wondered if they were happy. Or did they feel like they were in prison? Did they daydream of tunneling underground and escaping? Back to their home? I stood up and walked closer to the fence. One of the pandas moved closer. His face looked older than the others.

I thought to myself: that's gonna be you, Aiden. Caged and old and alone.

I felt so much sadness for him. I looked at his face and wondered if it was possible to have a happy life locked in a cage like that.

On the morning I was scheduled to meet back up with the agents, the phone scared me awake. The clock on the table read 8:15. I fumbled for the receiver and answered in a groggy mumble.

"Yeah?"

"Aiden. Agent Jackson. We're downstairs."

This was it. It was time. I threw on yesterday's clothes and stumbled down the steps and out the door into the morning light. It was already humid. A beautiful day. They were standing beside a civilian car. And I wanted nothing more than to tell them to go fuck themselves. Throw me in the can and toss the key. Let me rot. I ain't doing shit for you. I wanted to call their bluff. Grin and bear whatever consequences came.

But every time I mustered the courage to say it, I flashed back to the old panda in the cage. I didn't want to become that panda. I couldn't do it. I made up my mind in that moment. I would take their deal and become an informant.

We drove together about twenty minutes. Traffic was light. Just outside of town, the agents pulled into the back of a park with a fountain, a lake, and a play area for kids. The park was full of white yuppie parents pushing strollers and teenagers tossing a football. It's the kind of beautiful day I had seen a million times and taken for granted. But now, with my freedom slipping away, I wished I had slowed down to appreciate.

"Give any thought to our little offer?" Jackson asked, sipping his corner store coffee.

I nodded and took a deep breath. I couldn't reveal my hand too soon. I didn't wanna seem too eager. "If—and only if—I did decide to help you guys out, what kinda information would you need from me?"

Jackson took another sip and jerked his head toward a shady area with benches. We grabbed a table splattered in pigeon shit.

"You'd be what we call a confidential informant. You'd be working with the Department of Justice."

"But not for us," Douglas said. "You wouldn't be one of us."

"And what would I be doing? How dangerous is it?"

"You don't need to know the specifics of what you'll be doing," Jackson said.

I leaned in. "Do you guys know who we're talking about here? These are serious fuckin' guys. Do you wanna get me killed?"

"Aiden, this is a chance for you to start over," Jackson said. "To do something good with your life. Something you could be proud of."

Douglas piggybacked with a pitch of his own. "It could be a start of a whole new career for you. And who knows? Maybe someday you will be one of us."

"And my parents? They'd be protected too?"

"They wouldn't be implicated in crimes," Jackson said. "But this isn't witness protection. We're not responsible for keeping your family safe."

I dragged my hands over my face and took a sharp breath in. I could feel myself caving. I was going to become an informant. I told myself at the time I was doing it to protect my parents. I was doing it for my family.

But that wasn't the truth. The truth was: I was scared. I was eighteen and scared and just trying to survive.

"How does it work?"

"If you were to come on board, we'd need everything to look legit. We'd have to move slow and make sure there's no ripples. We'll figure out a way to get you out of school. You can't work for us and go to school at the same time. There's no way. Once we get you out, you'll be told where you'll be stationed and what your job will be. This isn't witness protection. We're not changing your name or relocating you. You're just gonna help us get some information."

"On who?"

"On whoever the fuck we say."

"And then what?"

"When you're done, you'll be free to go."

"And how the fuck do I know I can trust you."

"Maybe you can't. But what other choice do you have, Aiden?"

I closed my eyes. I nodded to myself one last time and told myself I was making the right choice. For myself. For my family. For my future.

"Okay," I said. "I'll do it. When do we get started?"

CHAPTER 3

The score was seven-nothing at the half. I came off the field with grass stains smeared on my kneepads and black field dirt under my fingernails. It was the first home game of the season. Thousands of die-hard locals filled one half of the bleachers, while the other was packed with folks from out of state, yelling and cheering from the stands. The cheerleaders were doing their high kicks, waving their pom-poms in a green and white blur.

I was playing for Michigan State. Off the whistle, Notre Dame fumbled the kickoff. Our ball. I took a knee at the forty-yard line, bit down on my mouth guard, and wiped the sweat that burned in my eyes. It was three p.m. on a Saturday afternoon. Hot beneath the Michigan sun, and humid as hell.

Our helmets knocked together in the muddy huddle as we listened for the play. The quarterback called for a simple run play. A moment later, I felt the sweat off the snap. I ran left, broke right, blocked the defensive tackle charging the center, but didn't see the linebacker coming up from behind. It was a beginner move I should've seen coming. But I didn't. I wasn't the same player I was a month ago. The linebacker sacked my QB, drilled him hard into the yellowing patchwork of grass. I saw Coach throw the towel. I heard the whistle from the sidelines.

"The fuck, Gabor? Where's your head at?" Coach Templeton shouted.

"Up your mother's twat," I yelled back.

"Keep it up, tough guy, and I'll bench you for the rest of your fuckin' life."

The bench was better than prison, I thought. I wanted to tell him exactly where my mind was. That it was a million miles away, suffocated with images of rotting away in a jail cell and even worse, thoughts of being found out by the friends I was about to flip on. That'd be a death sentence. A .38 against my temple and three rounds in my head on a random Wednesday after they find out I'm a snitch. Where's my mind? It was gone. But I'd been playing ball long enough to know the consequences that came from disobeying my coach, especially during a game, so I kept my mouth shut and played my part.

"Sorry, coach!" I yelled out. "My fault."

We huddled for second down. I had another chance. That was one of the things I loved most about football. There always seemed to be a second chance. You could fumble or fall or get sacked into oblivion. But there was always another play, another quarter, another game. Life wasn't always like that.

Hut! Marshall faked the handoff, tossed it to me instead, but the sweaty leather slipped out of my hands, and I dropped the ball. I quickly fell on the fumble for the recovery, but it was too late. I could see my coach jogging onto the field to pull me.

"I don't know where your head's at, Gabor, but you're out," he said. "Martinez is gonna cover." And with that, he benched me for the rest of the game.

I pulled my helmet off. The truth was, I was relieved. With a life sentence hanging over me, everything changed. Nothing seemed to matter. Least of all a football game. As I took off jogging back toward the locker room, I saw two men step through the field gate. It was them. The two Department of Justice agents. Agent Jackson and Agent Douglas. Jackson tilted his head up at me as we made eye contact. I slowed my jog and stood there on the sidelines with my hands on my hips and my chin dropped to my chest. They knew exactly where to find me. It was time to hear them out. We made plans to meet up first Monday morning.

Downtown Detroit was packed with civil servants rushing in a post-lunch panic to their sad little office gigs. At least that's what I thought at the time. I had always maintained a certain unreasonable contempt—you could call it disrespect—for that way of life. The white-collar cubicle dwellers. The men and woman who were satisfied to stand in line and wait their turn. The nine-to-fivers who toed the line. I never wanted to punch a clock or ask my manager permission to take a piss. The risks of running with Eddy came with one major reward that superseded everything else: with Eddy, you never had to wait in line.

Agent Jackson yanked the back door open and stepped out and stared upward, toward the top of the Department of Justice offices. What would Eddy be thinking if he could see me now? What would my father think? Or would they spit in disgust at the decision I made? Those questions tormented me as the agents led me through the revolving glass doors, through a green marble lobby, a metal detector, up the brass elevators, and into a windowless back room where they told me to wait and kept me waiting for hours, alone with my thoughts, with my doubts crushing down on me.

The room was off-white. A government-issued metal desk and a filing cabinet in the corner. The rugs looked like they hadn't been changed in twenty years. In the back corner, there were stacks of boxes.

Jackson and Douglas came into the room and took a seat in front of me. The waiting, I assumed, was a strategy, a way for them to get in my head and show me I wasn't a priority. They wanted me in my place.

"How ya been since we last spoke?"

"Not sleeping. Feel like shit."

"That's normal. There's a period of grieving that comes after something like this. You lost something. Even though nobody's died, it probably feels like it. Because in a way, your old life did die. And now you gotta adapt to this new one."

I shrugged off his attempt to psychoanalyze me. I tried to retain a blankness to my expression. I couldn't let them see behind my facade. I was still playing my cards close to my chest.

"Douglas and I been kicking around some ideas for you. What we need is somebody we can trust on the inside. We need you to join the police force. We need somebody who can be our eyes and ears. You get it?"

"A cop? You think you can trust me?"

"You tell me, Aiden. Can we?"

"Why would you?"

"Well, until you give us a good reason not to, we're gonna try. We need your help, and you need ours."

At that moment, Jackson reached into a duffel bag, dug around for a bit, and then casually tossed a fat white envelope on the table. I let it lie there a moment. I knew what it was. I'd held enough envelopes for Eddy to know.

"What's that?"

"That's for you, Aiden. Open it."

The lip of the envelope wasn't quite sealed, and I could tell just from the feel that it was thick with money. I peeked inside. There must've been at least five grand in crisp hundreds, twenties, fives. I paged my way through it, fingering my way through the bills, doing a quick count, silently moving my lips as I counted. Once I had the whole stack counted, I looked at them and furrowed my brow in confusion.

"I don't get it," I said.

Jackson leaned forward with his elbows propped on the table. "We need this to look legit. We can't have anybody questioning why you left school all of a sudden."

Douglas chimed in. "One day you're playing football and studying business. Then, all of a sudden, you disappear. And become a cop? Looks shady as hell."

"We need it to be for real. We need you to get kicked out of school."

"Is this a joke?"

I couldn't believe these two cops were suggesting something so reckless and irresponsible. It almost felt like a setup or prank.

"Your only job for the rest of this semester is to take that money and go fuckin' crazy with it. Party it up. Booze it up. Blow off classes. Do whatever it is you have to do to get tossed. Once you're on academic probation, you can bail, and we'll have a record of it. If anybody's watching, you'll just look like another fuckup kid."

I scoffed and shook my head and started laughing.

"You're serious?"

"Dead serious."

As I paged my way through the money one more time, Agent Jackson touched me on the hand and asked me: "What do you think, Aiden? Can you do it?"

"What happens after I flunk out?" I said.

The agents exchanged glances. "You're gonna join the police force."

"You want me to be a cop?"

"We need somebody on the inside, Aiden."

"How is being a cop gonna help you bust up the crew? They'll never trust me if I'm a cop."

And that's when they dropped the bombshell that changed everything. "We don't need you to help us bust your crew, Aiden. We need you to help us find corruption within the force."

I held my stare on his until he was forced to look away. "You want me to help you bust corrupt cops?"

"And you need to be a cop to do it."

My reasoning for accepting the assignment was a combination of fear and pragmatism. I left the DOJ office that day with a wad of dirty money and got on a bus. The first instinct I had was to run. Hop the next train back to Jersey and disappear into the old neighborhood. Or skip town on a red-eye flight to Brazil. Make a new life in some country without an extradition treaty with the States. Go find Eddy and restart the old crew.

I thought about it. Escaping. But I didn't have the nerve. So I took a local bus back to my campus. Back inside my stuffy dorm, I counted out the money into small stacks. I took a moment to process what was about to happen. There's no turning back once I decide to destroy my college record. I was putting my future, my life in their hands. And as little as I trusted them, I knew I couldn't face the alternative. An uncertain future was better than no future at all.

With five grand in my pocket and a free pass to piss my life down the toilet, the rest of the semester became a booze-addled blur. I spent most of the next three months in a drunken stumble haze, zigzagging around East Lansing, in and out of dive bars and frat parties. The drinking was a distraction. A painkiller. It took the shame away. I began inventing all kinds of ways to get in trouble. I drank and stole. I got into fist-fights in Irish pub parking lots. I'd drink whatever they gave me. Got tanked on cheap bourbon and bottom-shelf wine. My dorm room was a mess of empty bottles, forties, half-pints on ashtrays. I'd sleep until noon. Stay out until dusk. I blew off my business classes. Intro to Econ and Earth Science. It was all bullshit to me now.

Soon it was October, and I began seeking out parties, sneaking in and getting plastered. Any excuse I could think of to party and spend money, I took it. I drank at bars, in Greek houses, in my dorm, on the streets. Had sex with strange girls whose names I barely knew. I threw up in trash cans and tried to forget the mistakes I had made.

Eventually, after too many absences, the university bursar sent me a warning in the mail that I would soon be put on academic probation. Then another warning. Then another. I piled them up and set them on fire. There was nobody I could turn to that would help me to stop. I was alone with my problems. I was losing my mind. Out of control. Never in my life had I been so sad while having so much fun.

One night, after stumbling into my dorm after a long night of drinking, I woke up from a nightmare and caught myself staring at the ceiling and then at the football posters on the far side of the room, tacked up on the wall. I had stopped playing foot-ball, too. Stopped going to practice. I'd see my former teammates in the quad and avoid eye contact. This had been the worse part for me. For as long as I could remem-ber, it had been my dream to play pro ball in Tampa. And I began thinking back to what Agent Jackson had said about mourning the death of my former life. He was right. I'd been raging and boozing so hard, trying to forget, that I hadn't fully pro-cessed what I'd lost. The death of the person I thought I would someday be. That was

38

the hardest part of it all. Sometimes I'd wish they would just snuff me out in an alley. I wasn't scared to die. But taking away a person's dream? That was a different kind of torture.

That night, as I lay there letting it all wash over me, I decided to untack the football posters from the wall, one thumbtack at a time. I folded them up and slid them under my bed. That's not me, I said. That's not who I am. Not anymore. As much as it almost killed me, it was time to let go of the dream.

———

A couple months later, I went home for Christmas break. I had one thing to accomplish during Christmas back at home: to tell my parents I dropped out of school. Nothing much was different in the Bluffs, but nothing felt the same. I'd only been gone a few months, but an unperceivable shift had occurred. The city felt lonelier, emptier. The old neighborhood was the closest place that felt like home, but riding through the streets, something felt out of place.

My first night back, I stopped by my folks' house to drop off my bags. My father, as usual, was away at work at with the transnational train company where he'd worked for twenty years. And my mother was home with dinner on the stove, in her nightgown making Hungarian goulash and red potatoes. I hated that dish, had since I was a kid, but I never had the heart to tell her. I hugged my mother when I saw her, held her longer than I had in a while. Mixed up in all my feelings was the disappointment she was going to suffer when I told her I had gotten kicked out of school. All the sacrifices she had made for me, and I was meant to repay her by going to college and making a life for myself that my parents could only have dreamed of. Somewhere along the way, I'd broken that promise, and now I had to find the words to tell her.

That night, after a quiet dinner with my mother, I couldn't bring myself to tell her. Instead, we ate with the TV on, glancing occasionally at my father's empty seat at the head of table.

After my mother went to bed, I decided to meet up with a friend. I wanted one night to feel normal again—an escape to an easier time when I could go out with the boys and not feel the weight of the world crushing down on me. I borrowed her Lincoln Continental, filled up the tank, and drove back into the old neighborhood. The car garage was still there. The diners and bars we used to drink at hadn't changed.

But the crew was gone. New gangs had taken over the corners. The days of us running the streets were over.

I parked behind the dive bar. Inside, I saw my best friend, Joey Sasso, sitting at a high-top near the back.

The bar was cabin-wood paneled and decorated with sports pendants, newspaper clippings, and legend's jerseys from the neighborhood. It was a bar I used to come to with Eddy and the guys. They used to know me there.

Joey and I had been running packages for the DeCavalcante crew since we were twelve years old. We were two sixth graders collecting packages for one of the most dangerous men in the country before our balls had even dropped. He was a different sort of friend than Donnie Cooper, or even Sam. He was a friend I knew through the mob, and sharing those experiences drew us closer together. For an only child like me, having a friend like that meant everything. But there was one important detail that always separated us: Joey was Italian. To get made in the DeCavalcante crime family, you had to be Italian. If the crew ever got back together, Joey would have a real shot at climbing the ranks and getting made someday. That wasn't the case for me. I was a Hungarian kid who'd always been an outsider no matter how high I flew. I had always been a little jealous of that. No matter what, Joey always had the edge.

Still, he was one of my closest friends, and this would be the first time I'd have a chance to try out my cover story.

"Look who it is!" he said, with his arms opened wide. "College boy, back in town."

Joey had put on a little weight since I'd last seen him. The "college-boy" moniker was meant as a playful jab—none of the guys ever thought I'd make it to college. We spent an hour or two shooting the shit, throwing back Budweisers and reminiscing. When he finally asked about college, I deflected the question.

"C'mon, how's football?"

I took a big gulp of my beer, killed the bottle, and dropped the bomb on him.

"Actually, I decided college wasn't for me."

Joey tried to read my face, looking for clues, a smirk that I might be kidding. We'd pull ribs on each other all the time, and this probably sounded like a joke. But soon he saw the seriousness in my eyes and his face went somber.

"Not for you? Fuck does that mean?"

"C'mon, you know me. Can you see me taking fuckin' business courses?"

The disappointment that washed over him surprised me. Then it occurred to me, sitting there, that the guys from the street may have felt a certain amount of pride that one of their own had gone straight and made it with the civilians. And now I was taking that away from him.

"So what then? You gonna drop out?"

"Thinking about maybe joining the force."

"The force? Get outta here. What force?"

My silent stare told him everything he needed to know.

"The police force?" he asked. "You? No offense, Aiden, but you might actually be the last person on Earth I could see becoming a cop."

"There's a lot worse out there than me," I said.

"You sure about that?"

After another hour of catching up, Joey started warming to the idea of me being a cop. In our world, cops and wiseguys had similar interests: we cared about our neighborhoods and our families. We all wanted to make money. We just had very different perspectives and interpretations of the law. But the more we spoke, the more Joey realized it wouldn't be such a bad thing, having a friend like me in uniform. Soon, we paid our tab, twisted our cigarettes out into a glass ashtray, and hopped into Joey's car.

The house party was Joey's idea. He drove us to the north side to a house party in the Bluffs. The entire car ride, I was dreading running into anybody I knew. There was this unspoken sting of shame living inside me back then. It burned like stomach acid stuck in my chest. The truth was nobody ever thought I'd ever make it out of my neighborhood and into college. I was never much of a student. Because of my learning disabilities, they pegged me as a blue-collar dropout. They thought of me as the kind of guy who—if I was lucky—would grow up fixing rusting radiators. But most likely I'd wind up in jail. Or dead. Or living back home. When the crew dissolved, I knew football was my last shot to prove them all wrong. And for a short while, I thought I had. I got into Michigan State and shocked everybody. I could never forget the surprise that registered on their faces when they heard the news "You?" As if to say I wasn't good enough. It felt good to prove them wrong. To make it out on my own merit and show them I was more than what they thought I was.

But now, I was returning home not as a football hero but as a fallen gangster. I had become the thing they always knew I'd become. A part of me wanted them to know I wasn't some dropout or some disgraced mobster wannabe. I was more than all that. I was an informant now and someday I'd do something to help this city. The city deserved a noble police force, not one that was poisoned with corruption. I thought I could help make that a reality. But I couldn't say a word. For now, I had to swallow the shame and walk into the party as the dropout.

The crowd was a mix of young yuppies, guys I knew from high school who stuck around to waste away at community college, and a few of the wannabe gangsters from Eddy's old crew. I tried to keep a low profile. The kitchen was littered with empty Michelob bottles, liters of 7-Up, handles of warm vodka and Captain Morgan's, red plastic cups.

Across the room I saw a girl around my age on the patio outside. The memories I have of that moment, if they're to be trusted, are colored in golden light, as if the rest of the party went dark, lights dimmed, and this girl of my dreams in a strapless red dress dared me to try. I don't know how long I stood there staring, gawking, struck by her beauty, as if she were a rare artifact, like something you'd see in a museum. I was trying to build up my nerve. It had never taken me more than a split second to punch a guy. But to go up to a girl like that? I needed all the courage in the world. The bass from the music was blasting as I picked up my drink and elbowed my way through the crowded living room. I stepped onto the freezing patio where she was smoking with some friends. As I got closer to her, I could see she was out of my league, which only made me want to know her even more.

She said her name was Carrie. Said she'd seen me around. She knew me. Knew I used to run with Eddy, and I wondered to myself how I could've missed a woman who looked like her. Then, I saw some guy coming up in my periphery.

"Aiden," I heard him say. "Heard you flunked outta Michigan State. Now what?"

Without a second thought, I turned and shoved the guy hard in the chest. I knew there'd be jokes made at my expense, but I couldn't let him mock me in front of Carrie. My hands landed square of his chest. I hadn't bothered to even see who I was pushing, didn't realize how much bigger he was than me. His size worked against him as he stumbled backward into a table covered in party cups and spilled beer and Ping-Pong balls and the table shook and rattled, and everything spilled to the groans of the crowd around us.

"You know who you're laying hands on?" he said.

I didn't care. I could feel Carrie's eyes on me as this six-four punk took a wild swing. He missed but caught me with his left. I rocked him in the ribs with a shot, then another in the sternum as the crowd started yelling "fight!" Another heavy fist to the sternum and this big lug went down, keeled over to a knee. I smashed his face open with my forehead and he went down on his back. I stumbled, too, as the head-butt caught me and rattled my own brains.

His friends got between us before I could knock him out, and we were separated as they dragged him out into the front yard through the side gate. I sat in the living room with an ice pack on my swelling knuckles when I saw Carrie coming toward me. I was buzzed and fed up and didn't feel like being mocked.

When I looked back at Carrie, she wasn't startled at all. Her squinted eyes communicated something else altogether—that this singular act of violence triggered something inside of her. She looked as if she were attracted, even turned on, by my aggressiveness.

After that fight, I asked her for her number. She scribbled it down on a piece of paper and I kept it in my shirt pocket. I knew she was trouble, and she knew I was worse, but we couldn't resist.

My father came home two days before Christmas. I decided I didn't want to ruin their Christmas with the bad news, so I waited five more days to drop the bomb on them. For their safety, I couldn't tell them about my plea deal with the Department of Justice, so I needed to find a way to tell them I was going to become a cop without tripping their suspicions.

The morning of December 27, I took a long walk in the freezing cold, when it was still dark out, before the garbage trucks and bakeries and street sweepers. I had never been much of a sleeper, but from the moment those two DOJ agents turned my life upside down, I hardly slept at all. I'd close my eyes for two hours before I'd jolt awake. My sheets would be drenched in sweat. My dreams, whenever I could remember them, were like a flip-book from hell: falling, drowning, my teeth falling out into my palm.

That night at dinner, I had my story ready to go. My heart was pounding in my chest. I sat between my parents at the dining room table, pushing my food around on my plate. The only sound other than our chewing was coming from the TV news. It was the early eighties, and the newscaster was droning on about Reagan, the economy, the rising gas prices.

"Dad, how was work?"

"Work was work," he said. "Ready to retire. Your turn to earn some money. When you gonna sign one of those big NFL contracts?"

I took a bite of my chicken and let the sounds of the TV news fill the house. My mother had made her famous chicken dish, carrots, and a ginger broth stew. It was Christmastime, and the tree was lit up in the corner of our house. The lights played a holiday hymn and the lack of conversation underscored how little we had to say to each other.

"How are your classes, Aiden?" my mother asked.

"Good," I said. "They're good."

This was it. I had to tell them and if I didn't do it now, I may never muster the courage again. I set my fork down, ran my hands through my hair, took a deep breath, and plunged into the deep water.

"I have some news you're not gonna like," I said. I heard a quaver in my voice and tried to steady myself through breathing.

My father dropped his fork and leaned all his weight on one elbow. He shot me a look I'd seen a hundred times. I tried to look him in the eye but I couldn't. I fixed my eyes to the table and spoke: "I got kicked out of school," I said. "I flunked out."

My father erupted. "God fucking damn you, Aiden!" He slammed his hands down on the table and the wineglasses clattered and the silverware fell to the floor.

"Honey, relax," my mother said.

"Don't you tell me to relax," he said, standing. "The fuck's wrong with you? Huh? You know how hard we work? Your mother and me? And you can't even pass a few classes? What about football?"

"I quit," I said.

I'd heard stories about my father. I knew he'd been in his fair share of fights back when he was in Budapest, on the Pest side, running a street gang on the north side of the river. I'd seen him hurt before, but the words I'd just spoken—I quit—seemed to knock the wind out of him. He staggered back as if I had physically assaulted him. He didn't have any words for the letdown he was feeling.

"So what are you gonna do?" my mother asked.

"I decided to become a police officer."

"Oh, a police officer," my father said. "You believe this? A police officer? With your priors you think you're gonna be a cop? I wanna know who raised you. Because you're not acting like any son of mine."

"Dad, don't say that."

"You grew up in this neighborhood. Eddy raised you like a son. And now you come home and tell me you're gonna turn your back on everything you've ever known and become a fucking pig cop? Is that what you're telling me?"

I diverted my eyes down at the carpet. The sounds on the TV only served to trivialize everything that was happening between us. I looked him in the eye and held contact just long enough for him to say, "I don't ever wanna see your face again. You understand me? You disappoint me."

"I know," I said.

"Get your shit and get out. Don't say another word."

Outside, it was fourteen degrees and closing in on eleven o'clock when I made it on foot to the gas station. Inside the small convenience store, I bought a pack of smokes and a lottery ticket. Took a piss around back and slotted three quarters into the pay phone. After a few rings, the operator answered. I asked to be connected to a local cab, somebody that could take me to the train station. I waited for the taxi to arrive, to take me away from this city that was no longer my home, and into a new life, where I was no longer a criminal, but would never be a real cop.

CHAPTER 4

It was winter and cold, and the campus was quiet. I parked my silver Bonneville in the north lot reserved for Rutgers faculty and students, but I wasn't enrolled as either. I'd never be a student again. It was a year and change since my life was destroyed after I walked into my Michigan State dorm room and found two agents waiting for me. A couple months into my spring semester I was officially expelled from Michigan State and told to never return. It'd be years before I realized the full weight of that decision. But I chose to do it. I decided to save my own life, dropped out of school, and gambled on the Justice Department. The question was: Could I trust them?

It was barely six in the morning and the students were still asleep in their dorms. The early cold never fazed me. After years of playing football, I was used to waking up in the dark. By the library with the tall Corinthian columns, a campus cop nodded at me, pointed me to the west side. I followed blue signs staked into the grass that led the way to the police academy. The academy was headquartered in a small town just outside Newark, but they had classes on the Rutgers campus.

I was only twenty, a kid, though I felt much older, and worn out. But there was something familiar about the campus. I could almost trick myself into believing the police academy was offering me a second chance at the college experience I'd always wanted. Inside I knew things could never be the same.

The academy was twelve weeks of boot camp hell. A sadistic, three-headed snake of physical training, academic classes, and field training.

The gym smelled like rubber mats and dank, unventilated air. By seven, the room was packed with one hundred hopeful recruits. I knew half of the police hopefuls would never make it to the end. Like football drills, the cadet academy was designed to weed out the weak. It was an unintended coincidence of my time playing football, but I felt it had unintentionally trained me for this moment. I had been conditioned to survive.

Morning formation was at seven sharp. My name was third on the roll call list. The drill instructor was a big, surly man with his face hidden by mirrored sunglasses.

"Gabor!" he shouted.

"Here!" I shouted back, with the same bellow I reserved for football roll call.

The physical training drills brought me back to my football days, even though we weren't training on a field. We would begin in the dark with a half mile run down the suburban streets.

In mid-January, the leaves were dead on the ground. School was just barely back in session and the kids waved hello to us as we passed them on their way to school. All around us were working-class homes and brick factory facades and falling-down buildings and rusting water towers.

I hadn't run a football drill in over a year, but my mental toughness quickly kicked in and I was able to pace myself as we jogged in the cold air, lungs burning, around the corner and back, batons in our hands, while the instructor blew a whistle for us to hustle back to our pods on campus. In those first few hours, I began to feel as if all the training I'd done to become a pro football player was going to push me toward becoming a cop. My training, my athleticism, my thirst for combat. It seemed as if this had all been part of a divine plan.

After warm-ups, we gathered in the parking lot. We trained in the freezing cold. The instructors stalked past us, shouting in our faces like some blowhard caricatures from a military movie. Give me twenty push-ups. Fifteen jumping jacks. High knees. Twenty sit-ups. They had us dragging ninety-pound dummies a hundred yards and back.

Even on that first day, I saw the fatigue setting into those around me. Our shirts were soaked through with sweat. Cramps twisting like serrated knives in our ribs and sides. Aches went thrumming through our knees and joints. But my endurance was strong. I felt as if I'd been training my entire life for this.

Day two: the drill instructors kept the cadence as we marched through the streets. Left, right, left, right. Blowing their whistles to keep the stragglers from lagging. I was slowly getting to know the cadets. Every one of them had a different reason for joining the force. Some said it was their life's purpose and something about their virtuousness rubbed me the wrong way. Some were legacies—they were there because their fathers or uncles were cops. It ran in their blood. Some were simple, blue-collar types who wanted to make decent pay. And then there was me. I wondered if there was anyone else undercover, a secret criminal trying to save their own life with a last-ditch effort to stay out of prison. That was the biggest difference between me and everybody else. They chose to be there; I was there by force.

By the second week, the training had gotten more intense. We wore weighted vests to get used to running with a gun belt. I kept up as the difficulty increased and got into the swing of a routine.

After the morning drills, we'd shower off and meet back in the auditorium for the lecture series. Our classes were held in whatever spare room Rutgers had available. Each day, some higher-up on the squad would stand in front of the classroom and lecture about violent crimes, statistics, and unconscious bias in police work. We went over ordinary crime prevention methods but also events and scenarios I'd never considered, like patrolling mass protests and mayoral inaugurations or how to issue parking tickets.

During one of the seminars, a logistics expert came in and began talking to us about organized crime. As patrol cops it was made clear to us that we would rarely be called in for major investigations, but it was important for us to know the chain of command and how local police officers interacted with FBI and DEA agents. As they went on about the Mafia, I felt an uneasy stirring in my belly. A part of me felt like a traitor. I came from a world where cops were hated. I knew cops to be dirty, to be bullies, to be elitists. I couldn't help but look at the door from time to time and see the ghost of Eddy.

But part of me was drawn to crime, even on the other side of it. They had us studying laws and penal codes: the minutiae of police life. And while I was never much of a student, I found myself gravitating to this information in a way I never had with school. Something was shifting inside of me like numbers in a lock tumbler. I was getting close to figuring out my reason for being on this planet.

———

One Friday, sometime around the third week, we filed into a wide-open hall while the instructor wheeled a television set to the center of the stage. He dimmed the lights. A dozen cadets had already left the program and I looked around the room wondering who would crack next. On the screen: dash cam footage from a high-speed chase. I never paid too much attention to these class movies—they were always a decent excuse to rest my eyes in the dark, but there was something different about this one. As I sat in near darkness watching the cops speed after a stolen car, flooring it through intersections in broad daylight, it brought me back to my days stealing cars for Eddy.

"That could be me," I said, under my breath to nobody. I leaned forward in my chair and watched the harrowing footage. My pulse quickened as the cops sped after this stolen car. It was eerily reminiscent of a chase I'd once gotten in. I shuddered in my seat. My fingernails dug into my knees. The chase quickly went fatally wrong, and the driver ended up exploding his car into a tree. The dash cam footage ended in static, and the teacher hit the lights. I was still and stone-faced in my seat.

In those moments, when I was caught up in the adrenaline of the theft, I had never stopped to considered how close to death or prison I was. And there was another thing I'd never considered: I was putting the lives of those cops and citizens at stake. So many people could've gotten killed because of what I was doing for a little extra cash. That's not the person I wanted to be. As the lights came up, I was struck with a shock wave of self-awareness I'd never felt before.

It was me. I had been the problem. And now I was being trained to keep guys just like me off the street. In a strange way, there was a certain kind of relief in knowing that.

I became a model student. Nights were spent studying in my seventh-floor dorm. Dyslexia be damned, I was determined to learn every law, ordinance, and penal code in the county. I'd be in there for hours, downing mugs of black coffee, memorizing the statutes, shutting my eyes tight when the numbers and letters became a jumbled blur. I'd only break to sleep or eat.

I had made some friends in the squad by then, but I chose to keep a low profile. After a year of partying and getting trashed and thrown out of school I didn't have much of an appetite left for booze or parties or fun.

Something had changed inside of me after my last visit home too. Maybe it was the fight with my father or the way the old gang laughed at me when I told them I wanted to become a cop. Whatever it was it felt irreversible. I had something to prove. To them. To myself.

Some nights I'd call my new girlfriend, Carrie, who still lived in my hometown.

Over the last year we'd been dating off and on. Then, just before I left for the academy, she officially became my girlfriend. The long distance put a strain on us from the start and training took up most of my time, but I would call her when I had a chance and fill her in on everything I was learning. I thought I was in love, but I didn't really know her. Shallow as it may seem, she was a knockout, and it made me proud to have a girl like her on my arm. To make things work, I told myself she was everything I wanted her to be. Sometimes people are drawn to each other for reasons they can never explain. Sometimes those reasons turn about to be toxic. So, like a moth to a flame, I went into a relationship I knew nothing about that'd eventually have a painful ending.

———

But I didn't see much of Carrie in those days. I didn't see much of anybody. And loneliness began to take its toll. It didn't help that I was harboring a secret that I couldn't tell anyone. And the act of holding that painful truth inside had begun to suffocate me. I felt as if I had a boulder on my chest every second of every day. I got ulcers. I had dark suicidal thoughts. My thoughts were growing darker and sometimes I'd walk around the campus quad and watch the students pass by and wallow in my own missed chances. They seemed so carefree, bullshitting with each other, horsing around. I was only a year or so older than they were, but my body and mind felt ancient.

I'd shuffle my way back to my dorm and lie in the dark, wondering why I was even still here on this planet. At any point, I knew I could swallow a handful of pills and this all would be over. When I reached that most suicidal moment, my mother's face appeared in my mind's eye. As much as I wanted to be free of the pain, I could never put her through that sort of torment. And then another thought occurred to me: at twenty, I had already avoided death so many times, maybe God had a plan for me. Maybe I was here for a reason.

———

We were four weeks in, and another ten cadets dropped out. They were burnt out, mentally and physically. And while I was exhausted, I felt steady, too.

That week we also began firearm training. The gun range was in an empty brick warehouse close to the college campus. Inside it smelled like sawdust and munition smoke and sweaty gunmetal. There I stood, in the center of the gun range holding an unloaded .357 Magnum. I'd been the enforcer for Eddy Tocino for three years. This wasn't new to me.

I was thirteen years old the first time I held a gun. I'd been bullshitting with some of the crew bosses behind Eddy's auto shop, when Eddy himself came out with a gift:

a shiny Glock nine. I thought it might feel like a football, but it was heavier. The gun felt like a cannon in my hands as I pointed it.

"Wow, careful!" he said, moving behind me, adjusting my shoulders and my hips, like a father fixing his son's batting stance in Little League. I mimicked his movements as he showed me the proper way to plant my feet into the ground and hold the gun out straight and fire. I felt the pull of conflicting loyalties inside my chest: I wanted to impress Eddy but was hesitant, terrified even, to pull the trigger. I wasn't sure if I was even strong enough to do it—but there was something else stopping me, too. Even at thirteen, I knew there was an unpredictability to bullets. Could it ricochet off the pavement into my eye? Or what if went soaring into a neighbor's backyard and struck a child? These thoughts raced through my mind, and I almost didn't shoot. But I wanted to impress Eddy, so I pulled the trigger. I was launched backward from the blast. I couldn't believe the power of the gun. The sense of power it gave me was addicting.

I began practicing in the alleyway. I'd set up empty beer bottles on garbage barrel lids, turn the gun sideways, just like I saw the gangsters do in the movies. Then I'd throw my entire shoulder into it, shooting like I was throwing a football. Very few of the guys in Eddy's crew were trained shooters so we taught ourselves everything we knew. Nobody could tell us any different.

Now, in the gun range, wearing earmuffs and safety goggles, I stood in my section, aiming for the target down the aisle, while the range master studied my technique. After a moment, he stopped me.

"What the hell are you doing?" he said. "You'll break your wrist shooting a gun like that, and you'll never hit shit."

It was in that moment that I learned there was an art to shooting.

The instructor stood behind me. He taught me proper hand and foot placement, how to stare down the gun's scope, how to properly aim and protect my joints with each shot. As I popped off my first round, I saw bullet holes erupt in a circle around the target's torso. With an approving nod, he took the gun from me and showed me how to make some slight adjustments to my form. The experience was enlightening, but it also went a long way in building my respect for the skill and training police officers went through.

As I left the gun range, I wondered what Sarge would think if he knew who I really was. He was training a former mob enforcer how to use a firearm. And what about the agents at the Department of Justice? They were teaching a known criminal every trick in their book. I realized in that moment that they were gambling on me just as much as I was gambling on them.

The next eight weeks passed by in a blur. Week after week, I muscled through the new challenges. I was teargassed and handcuffed and wrestled to the ground in the rain. I struggled through written tests and read more dense police code than I ever thought I would need in my life. I did a couple ride alongs and shadowed real police officers to get a sense of how they worked in the field.

Then, at the end of the twelve weeks, I was one of only fifty cadets left of the hundred who enrolled to receive the honor of being a police officer. Starting pay was $19,800, about the same amount I'd make stealing one car for Eddy. But this wasn't about money anymore.

Graduation day fell on a quiet Sunday morning. It was a clear day in April, and the sky seemed to be more open than I ever remember seeing it. The ceremony was held inside the Eisenhower Auditorium in the center of the Rutgers campus. Parents arrived early carrying flowers and greeting cards. The theater fit about three hundred and as I sat in the front row in my police blues, I kept turning to stare at the door, waiting for my mother to arrive. When she finally ducked through the door holding yellow flowers, I rushed up the stairs to greet her. I was proud to be a mama's boy and I hugged her. But the feeling was immediately darkened by the absence of my father. I didn't have any delusions of the man—I knew he was as stubborn as I was, and my mother had already warned me that he wasn't going to show. But a part of me still held out hope that he'd arrive to watch me walk.

Even without my father, I felt proud to have finished. Up until that moment my life had been a series of false starts and unfulfilled dreams. I thought I'd be a football star, but my dreams were thwarted by the Department of Justice. I had imagined a life in business, but that never panned out. There was a time I thought I'd be a career criminal, the right-hand man of Eddy Tocino, but even that fell apart. I sat in that chair on graduation day and felt as if I had finally found my calling. I'd finished what I started. I was a cop and nobody could ever take that away from me.

After the ceremony, my mother and I went to dinner at a small Italian restaurant on a side street near campus. We ate slowly and mostly without speaking. Through the years, my mother was the most consistent person in my life. She showed up for me. As we ate, there was a feeling that something was going unsaid.

"How's Dad doing?" I finally said.

"Your father's fine," she said. "Working all the time."

"As usual, huh?"

"He asks about you," she said. "He asks how you're doing."

"It's none of his damn business."

My mother looked down and exhaled slowly. She was trapped between her husband and her son, and she knew we were two of the most stubborn men in the world. I think she was worried we might never speak again and it scared her. Or maybe it scared me.

"He doesn't really understand why you're doing this—this whole cop charade."

I wanted to tell her the truth. To keep a secret this heavy was causing my chest and stomach to burn. But for her protection—and my own—I knew I had to keep it inside.

"It's not a charade, Ma. It's my job."

"But why? It's dangerous. You're gonna get yourself killed, you ask me."

"Can we change the subject?" I asked, putting down my fork.

"Fine," she said. "So where's that girlfriend of yours? She doesn't show up on your big day?"

The topic of Carrie was a tense one for my mother. She had only met Carrie once and didn't think much of her. I was too deep in the love fog to see the red flags my mother saw. She wasn't afraid to voice her opinion on the topic.

"C'mon, Ma, it's a long drive out from the Bluffs. She's working."

"Working . . . " she said."

"C'mon, Ma, give the girl a chance. You barely know her and you already hate her."

"Mothers know," she said.

———

A few weeks later, on a rainy Saturday morning, I was on the phone with Carrie, planning a time to meet up that weekend. It would be the first Saturday in months I'd get to see her. She casually asked what I was doing with the rest of my day, and I lied. I told her I was picking up an extra shift, covering for one of the boys, when the truth was starkly different: I was driving an hour outside of Newark to a diner to meet Agent Jackson.

I felt Carrie was starting to pick up in the small inconsistencies in my stories. All those little untruths began to add up, and I saw a distrust begin to grow between us. I was too distracted by the DOJ to worry about it, though.

It's a short drive to Newark. As I drove, the rain slowed to a drizzle, and I took a moment to consider the meeting I was about to walk into. Ever since I had agreed to go undercover, the agents had been tight-lipped about my purpose. They told me only the most essential information over months of training, always keeping me on the hook. After being kept in the dark for months, I knew I would be informing on suspected corrupt police officials, but I didn't know who, or why, or even how. But now, at last, I felt I was going to receive my first official assignment.

At a quarter past noon, I pulled my Bonneville into the parking lot of a Howard Johnson's—the diner chain had become our unofficial office for these clandestine meetings. Jackson was already waiting for me in a booth near the back. The diner was choked in stale cigarette smoke, and I could see Jackson twisting out his cigarette as I made my way through the restaurant.

"Thanks for making the drive," Jackson said as I sat down. "Want some coffee?"

I shook my head no. "Let's just get on with it."

Sitting there in that moment, I felt a dynamic shift between us. Before, I felt like a captive, a criminal forced to inform or suffer the consequences of prison. But now I was a police officer. Regardless of how I got there, I was an officially recognized cop, and that meant I had certain rights and certain standing. Agent Jackson didn't feel like my captor anymore—he began to feel like my colleague.

"How's the first couple weeks on the force been?"

I took a second to think about the question. "Been shadowing a vet," I said. "Most of our collars so far have been domestic disputes. Nothing too major yet."

"Cats in trees," Jackson said, nodding with a knowing look on his face. "The important thing right now is that they think you're one of them. You work hard, put in the hours, and nobody will suspect a thing."

I nodded.

"What have you heard about a guy named Terry McPhearson?"

Terry McPhearson. I had crossed paths with Terry way back, when I was working with Eddy. I'd seen him around and he probably pegged me as a fuckup kid but not as an official member of the crew. I took him for a typical workaday cop, and when I saw him around the precinct, I could tell he found my face familiar without being able to fully place it. He probably saw a lot of guys like me. Our schedules rarely aligned and I hadn't had a chance to fully connect with him in the few short weeks I'd been on the force.

Terry looked like a high school geometry teacher, with wide eyes and a generous smile. To me, he blended in with the rest of the uniforms and didn't stand out in any way. I couldn't understand why Jackson would be asking me about Terry unless it was to make small talk.

"Terry?' I said. "Nice guy. Normal, I don't know. Why?"

Jackson paused and sipped his coffee. I could tell he was trying to formulate his thoughts, but the longer he took, the more serious the situation became. He dragged his hands over his face. There was something he had to tell me he didn't want to.

"Terry's not the guy you think he is," he said. "We have reason to suspect he's working freelance as a hit man."

"Terry?" I blurted out. "Get the fuck outta here. Guy looks like a door-to-door Bible salesman."

But Jackson didn't smirk. His face didn't budge at all, and I could tell he was dead serious. Terry had been living in plain sight for years, a stand-up citizen and a respected vet with a badge. Jackson suspected that Terry was a dirty patrol cop who'd been hired as a hit man to execute a guy who owed them money. He blew the guy's brains out all over the dashboard and, conveniently, was the first cop on the scene of his own crime. Jackson also suspected Terry had executed a couple others, as the pattern of shooting fit, but they didn't have enough evidence to take him down.

I sat back in stunned silence.

"He may not look it, but Terry is a dangerous guy," he said. "We need you to get close to him. Take your time. Make him believe you're his friend. We need to know what he's done and when he's planning on striking next."

All this time, I had been waiting for my first major assignment, and now, I was about to step in front of a hit man's scope. There was no way I could say no. So I nodded. I'd just agreed to befriend a hired assassin. And in that moment, an image flashed across my mind's eye. I was lying in a pool of blood, covered in shell casings. Had I traded a life in a prison cell for an early trip to the grave?

"I think I can do it," I said.

CHAPTER 5

Terry was the target. A police officer suspected of sniping citizens as a side gig. Beloved cop turned contract killer on his day off. My mission was seemingly simple but potentially fatal. I needed to get close to him and gather as much information as humanly possible.

During my first few months on the force, I had very little interaction with Terry. By the time I arrived, the guy had been on the force a couple years and already he'd picked up the classic shit-don't-stink attitude. Like he was somehow better than the rest of us. Judging by looks alone, you'd never finger Terry as a killer. The agents may have suspected him of being a hit man for hire, but I sure as hell couldn't see him as a heavy. To me, the guy looked, acted, and dressed like a high school geometry teacher. He walked with his shoulders slouched—probably from the nine-hundred-pound chip on his shoulder. Short, stocky. Black hair thinning on top. He was so physically unintimidating that I grew to believe he pulled an abrasive, untrusting attitude to make up for what he lacked in size. For the life of me I couldn't imagine this meek little man blowing people away on contract. Then again, it's always the ones you'd never suspect.

Blue Bell, the town we patrolled, was sleepy and small: call it twenty thousand people on a good year. And the police force hired to protect it was small too, with only fifteen officers and seven patrol vehicles. On a busy weekend, you might see all seven patrol cars in use. Most of the crimes we responded to were domestic disputes. We worked in rotating shifts of two-men crews, and because the precinct was so intimate, it was just a matter of time before you partnered up with everybody.

About six months into my time on the force, I finally got paired up with Terry. It was a lucky break, and I knew I had to use my time wisely and do everything I could to find out who this guy really was.

———

The dispatcher's voice came crashing through static. *We got a 10-100. Civil distur-bance. Early forties male. Says his wife is assaulting him with a spatula.* Then we lost the signal to a hiss of white noise. As I fiddled with the frequency dial, the dispatcher's voice returned to spit out the address. Third night in a row, it was the same: 1350 N. Helmsfield Road.

"Jesus Christ," I said, dragging my hands over my face. "Not again."

"Only couple I know who fights more than me and my wife," Terry said. The call was for a married couple who'd been at war these last few days. She was a drunk and he was a cheater. Bad combination. Lucky for us they didn't own any guns or one of them would've been dead by now. In place of a firearm, the wife preferred chucking kitchen utensils at her husband's head. Sometimes it was saucepans and coffeepots and dish racks. One time it was an entire drawer of knives. Tonight, it was a spatula.

When the call came in, Terry and I were just killing time. Eating dinner in an empty lot outside a fast-food joint. Terry thought they had the best burgers in town. By this point I had already done a few shifts with the guy. We had started to develop a rapport.

Building trust takes time. With Terry, it required something else: street cred and some demonstrated proof that I was more than just some empty-headed rookie. If the agents were right, and he did have some murderous secret buried inside of him, it was stashed in a lockbox in his mind. Finding the key to unlock it would take more than patience—I had to figure out the code to the safe.

Our friendship developed gradually, over small conversations and subtle gestures. I knew that for him to feel comfortable opening up to me, I would have to do the same for him. Every night we were out there as partners, risking our lives together, wasting the hours together, I witnessed our camaraderie develop.

Soon an after-work routine developed. We would finish our shifts, change out of uniforms, and hit the bars and pizza joints. Two months after being paired, Terry finally spilled.

———————

We were throwing darts at Giomotti's Pizza. Off-duty comedown blues. In 1987, the joint was a still a cop dive: smoggy yellow light choked with smoke from Camels and Kools. Low, claustrophobic ceilings and fake wood paneling. Corridors tacked with Eagles pennants. The glory years. An entire city stuck in the past. College kids

cluttered by the pool table, racking up billiard balls, tossing down dollars by the side
pockets, gambling away their financial aid. Others huddled 'round the jukebox, slot-
ting in quarters for Queen and the Stones. Occasionally some douchebag would play
Blondie and bring the whole bar down. Near the back's where the senior cops holed
up, crying in their beers, up to their elbows in alimony. Terry and I finished our game
and grabbed two seats sat at the bar, scarfing down slices, bullshitting while his wife,
Diane, was in the bathroom.

It was barely eight-thirty, but Terry was already half in the bag. I was alternating
beer with water, pretending to be drunker than I was. Beneath a cracked pane of glass
on the bar counter were rows of marked-up bills and bottle caps, doodled on and
defaced. The dollar bills stared back at us and the conversation turned to money.

"Lemme ask you something," he said, a slight slur to his voice. "What made you
wanna join the force?"

"Why not?" I said with a shrug.

"Shit money," he said. "Shit hours. Shit work."

I could tell he was prying a bit, and I had a sound strategy when it came to Terry:
I'd share bits about my life in the hopes that he'd interpret my openness as a gesture
to share bits of his own. Sharing can be contagious, especially around guarded men
who rarely get the opportunity to do. And I never took my eyes off the ultimate goal,
never stopped reminding myself of one thing: Terry was the target.

"I was trying to make the football thing happen," I said, "but I blew out my knee.
College was a bust. What else was I gonna do?"

He finished gulping down his beer till there was nothing but white foam left.

"It's a decent gig," he said. "Don't get me wrong. You just don't seem the type."

"What type is that?"

"I don't meet many rookies who used to run with mob capos."

I smiled.

"Ancient history."

The bartender interrupted to ask if we wanted another round. "We'll do this again,"
he said, referring to the beers. "Put it on my tab." Terry was a regular. He knew the
bartenders, the waitresses, the indebted Eagles fans who gambled their kid's college
funds on the games. The way he spent money was my first clue he was killing on a
contract, but these were just hunches. I needed actual proof.

"So, how'd you get mixed up with those guys?" he asked. "Eddy and his crew."

"C'mon," I said, trying to deflect. "Leave that shit in the past."

"We're just talking here."

There was something different about his curiosity about my mob ties this time. His interest was more than casual—he was digging for something, but I couldn't tell what. But I recognized that sparkle in his eye—it was a fascination some people had with the Mafia. I knew it when I saw it and Terry had it. It was the sign of man who'd spent too many years toeing the line, doing what he was told. Guys like Terry lived vicariously through gangsters, and I knew why—men who never had respect will settle for fear. That was Terry. And sometimes that desire went beyond the vicarious. Sometimes it materialized into weak men turning to the dark side in a desperate attempt to regain control over their own lives. That evil glint in his eye told me everything I needed to know. The guy had it in him to be a killer. Now I just needed to find a way to coax it out of him. So in hopes that by revealing my own dark past, he'd reveal his own, I started talking.

"Eddy was a friend of my dad's," I said. "The two of them went way back, and I grew up with Eddy coming over to the house. He was practically an extension of my family, like a surrogate uncle."

"Your dad involved too?"

"Not here in Jersey, no," I said. "Back in Budapest he ran a small crew. Regional stuff, nothing like Eddy was doing here. But stateside, he went legit."

"But it's in your blood?"

I locked eyes with him. "You could say that."

"You musta gotten started pretty young."

"What's all this about?" I said. "You writing a book report?"

"Just interested in that world," he said. "You know, mobsters and cops, we ain't so different. So many fuckin' hypocrites on the force. Real pieces of shit. Some of these guys like to act like their shit don't stink, but they'll be selling dope on the side."

I nodded.

"Twelve," I said. "By sixteen I was swiping cars."

"Gotcha. But you never . . . "

His voice trailed off and he swigged his beer, but he didn't have to finish the sentence. I knew what he wanted to ask: Have you ever killed somebody? It was hard for him to utter the question—it was hard for anyone. I suspected it was because, deep down, nobody wanted to really know the answer.

"Nah," I said. "It never came to that."

He nodded and fixed his eyes to the floor.

"That's where the real money is," he said.

Terry was right. Hit men for hire could rake in thousands for a clean kill. It was a dangerous job that only a few people could carry out. You needed a special combination of skill and savvy to commit the murder without getting caught and a terrifying lack of empathy to do it without feeling. But before I could push him further on what he'd just said, I saw his wife, Diane, from the corner of my eye, making her way back to the table. Diane was his second wife—a leggy blonde who liked to wear comfortable clothes—a jeans and T-shirts kind of girl. Far as I could tell, drinking was all they had in common.

At the same time she was zigzagging her way through the tabletops, two guys walked in and swished passed her. She glanced for a second at the taller one. I saw it; Terry saw it. It was just a split second of a glance. Any other couple, on any other night, it would've been nothing, but Terry seemed to always be looking for a fight; I could tell, with that simple, innocent glance, she'd just handed her husband a gas can.

She slid back into the booth.

"Played 'Thunderstruck' for you, babe," she said. Diane was a knockout — blonde, full lips, wide hips, pretty face. She was out of Terry's league, and he knew it, which only served to deepen his jealousy. Terry was squinting at her, totally galled by what he'd just seen. Then, after a long tense minute, he spoke.

"You looking at that guy over there?" Terry said to his wife.

"What?" Diane said, genuinely confused by what she was hearing. "Get outta here with that shit."

"With what shit?"

"I wasn't looking at anybody. You're delusional."

"Oh, I'm delusional?" he said. "Tell me you weren't just looking over there. That guy there. The tall one. You think he's cute? Got some kinda crush on him or something?"

"A crush? I don't even know the man."

"Then why you looking?"

"Terry, I wasn't looking at anybody, baby! I went to the jukebox to play your favorite song for you. That's all."

"So I'm imagining things? You calling me a liar?"

"Jesus Christ! I wasn't looking. Ask Aiden."

Terry turned to me and asked point-blank: "You see her look at that guy?"

As I sat there trying to figure out what to say, something occurred to me: Diane could be the key to it all. The chaotic, toxic relationship they were trapped inside of was the opening I needed to learn the truth about Terry. One second, they were in sexual thrall with each other—the next he was threatening to kill her. It was a dynamic built on a contradiction—defined by swings of unconditional trust, then destroyed by extremes of fear and doubt. Since they were married, I thought it possible that Diane knew the truth about what he'd done. If I couldn't get it out of Terry, maybe I could get her to talk. Maybe his wife was the key to it all.

I sipped my beer and answered cautiously. "I honestly didn't see anything," I said. I needed Diane to like me, to trust me, and figured Terry was so drunk he wouldn't remember anything by the morning anyway.

"Why don't we just take a deep breath," I said.

An hour later, and we took the party back to Terry's place. Kept drinking until one in the morning. Playing five-card stud on his patio with the radio blasting too loud. It was almost as if he was daring his neighbors to ask him to turn it down. Around one-thirty, Diane called it a night. She stumbled up the stairs, but Terry wanted to keep going, drinking till he was bombed on the porch. We shared a bit more about our childhoods, our parents, some of the trouble we'd gotten into before we both joined the force.

"I think I'm gonna head out," I finally said. "Carrie's at home waiting for me."

Terry was slouched in his chair, eyes floating in his head. When he drank, he seemed to swing from anger to depression, from rage to loneliness, and as he nodded off, the booze seemed to be taking him to a dark place in his mind. As I got up to leave, I heard him mutter something indecipherable, though I caught just enough of it to turn around.

He said, "I've done it, you know."

"Done what?"

Terry sat up and leaned forward in his chair.

"Can I trust you?"

I sat back down. "If you can't trust your partner, who can you trust?"

Terry gulped down the rest of his beer and crushed the can in his hand.

"I've done it," he said, making a gun out of his finger and holding it to his temple. "I sent a guy to the big farm in the sky."

"You mean on-duty? With your service weapon?"

He shook his head no and smiled.

"Bullshit."

"No bullshit."

The only reason I could figure for him telling me was this: the guy's insecurity outweighed his intelligence. He needed to be liked, to be feared, probably to make up for getting picked on at the playground. He wanted me to know he could do something illegal and murderous. Maybe he thought it would change the way I looked at him. So, he bragged about shit you never say out loud. It wasn't enough for him to kill someone and get paid. The act wasn't complete until he bragged to his friends about it. He wanted me to know what a tough guy he was.

It was a trend I had seen when I was running with Eddy: damn near all sociopaths have the desire to take credit for their crimes. It wasn't logical or strategic. It was ego. It was machismo. And all I had to do was be patient while he gave himself away.

"Who?"

"Can't tell you that."

"Because you're full of shit," I said. "I grew up around buttons who made their name clipping guys. They had a vacant look in their eyes that you don't have."

The tactic wasn't flashy, but I had to try. I thought if I denied his ability, he'd feel egged on enough to reveal more. His safety was superseded by neediness, and I was trying to exploit it.

"His name was Muller," he said, ashing his cigarette into the plastic tray. "Some fuckin' deadbeat nobody. You know, one of these degenerate gambler types."

"Muller?"

"Mark Muller," he said. "Made more for that one job than I do an entire year on the force. It was in the papers."

Then he started chuckling to himself, as if he had a hilarious secret.

"The fuck's so funny?"

"I was the first cop on the scene," he said. "I popped this fuckin' guy. Went home. Changed into my uniform. And showed up on the scene."

I needed him to know he could trust me.

"Jesus Christ," I said. "That's hilarious. You showed up at the scene of the murder you committed? That's the funniest shit I ever heard."

"I'm sure that's nothing compared to the stuff you've seen," he said.

"Well, there is a small difference," I said.

"Yeah, what's that?"

"We were criminals," I said. "You're a cop. You took an oath to protect people. That's the difference."

———————

I woke the next morning with a throbbing in my temples. The kind of hangover that blurs your eyes, feels like someone's grinding their knuckles into the crown of your skull. Carrie was beside me in bed. Pretty little thing sprawled out in her nightgown, taking up more than half the bed, as usual. We'd been dating about a little over a year at that point. On again, off again. Long-distance for the most of it. But ever since I joined the force, we'd become a bit more serious. At eight a.m., she was still asleep, her blonde hair in a messy tangle and her face covered by a pillow to keep the sunlight from her eyes. I sat up and dry swallowed four aspirin. Then I grabbed my pocket notebook and scribbled down everything I could remember about the conversation with Terry. Names, dates, details.

I used the kitchen phone to call Agent Jackson. Told him I needed to meet with him urgently. Today if he could swing it. It was about Terry. As soon as I hung up with Jackson, Carrie came shuffling into the kitchen in her slippers, wearing one of my oversized football practice shirts that covered her to the middle of her thigh.

"Who was that?" she said, looking in the fridge for some orange juice.

"That was work," I said, lying to her. "They want me to come in."

"It's your day off, baby. I thought we were gonna go to my sister's today."

"I can't today," I told her. "Maybe next weekend."

"That's what you said last weekend."

There was a part of me that wanted to tell Carrie about the secret other life as a DOJ informant—but I couldn't trust her. Not yet. Looking back, my relationship with Carrie was as illogical as most young love is. Similar to Terry and his wife, Diane, we had two modes: sex and fighting. It was a toxic loop, but one I felt compelled to perpetuate. Call it "moth to a flame" but it was stronger than that. It was love as I understood love to be at twenty-one years old. And the truth was, after losing Eddy, and losing my father, and losing the crew, and losing football, I was desperate to be a part of something where I wasn't all alone. If I couldn't join someone else's family, I wanted to start one of my own. In Carrie, I thought I'd found that person.

That afternoon, I drove my Bonneville to a town outside of Newark, close to the DOJ headquarters. I was growing tired of these long-haul trips to meet the agents, but it was the only way to keep my identity safe. There was a small part of me that was worried Terry would wake up the next morning paranoid about what he'd told me. Would he panic and threaten me? Or did he really trust me enough to share something so dangerous? Only time would tell. A short while later, I arrived in Newark and saw Agent Jackson sitting, smoking on a park bench.

"You know, I'm gonna need a second job just to pay for gas," I said. "You know what it costs me to get down here twice a month? Why don't I just get an apartment down here already?"

"Is that why you drove down here?" he asked. "To complain about gas prices? Or do you have something for me?"

"What if I said I had a confession?"

He stopped cold.

"I'd say it would be stupid to joke around with something as serious as that."

"Not a joke," I said. "Turns out, Terry ain't playing with a full deck. Guy's got such a hard-on to be one of the boys he's willing to go around bragging about his murders."

"He told you he killed someone? He said those words?"

I nodded.

"And he just told you? Just like that?"

"Don't make it sound so easy," I said. "I'm risking my balls out there for you. But the guy trusts me. He told me point-blank he killed some guy named Mark Muller. That your guy?"

"He told you about Muller?"

I nodded.

"And you got it on tape?"

"No, I wasn't expecting him to say shit. I thought we were just going out for a couple beers. I didn't know he was gonna spill his guts like an idiot."

Jackson dragged his hands over his face as if he were trying to rip his flesh off.

"We need it on tape, Aiden," he said. "If we don't have a recording, it's inadmissible in court. I can't go in there with this he said/he said shit. We gotta have it concrete or it's nothing."

"You're shitting me. The fuckin' guy told me he did it. Run his prints. Bring him in for questioning."

"It's not that simple, Aiden. The judge is gonna need to hear the confession. He's not just gonna take our word for it."

The following weekend, I made another trip to Newark. The black Lincoln of Agent Jackson was getting pelted with rain, idling in the torrential downpour, coughing out black smoke. I pulled my car next to his and held a newspaper over my head as I opened the passenger-side door and ducked inside. He handed me a pen.

"What's this?" I said.

"It's your recording device," he said.

It looked just like an ordinary retractable pen, but when I pressed my thumb into the spring-loaded ink cartridge, a tiny red light went on to indicate it was recording. He told me it had the capacity to record up to twenty-five hours. I could click it on before I went out with Terry and Diane and let it roll. The trick was to have it somewhere in front of them when they were speaking, so as not to risk obscuring their voices.

I paused and looked down at the device as my heart began to race. "Don't you think a guy like Terry will know what this is?" I asked. After all, he was a seasoned cop with a suspicious mind. At the same time, there were nights he got so sloshed he could barely remember what planet he was on.

"Let's hope not," said Agent Jackson. "The last thing I want is to be cleaning your brains off a sidewalk."

The pen was clipped inside my shirt pocket for the next couple weeks. Terry and I kept getting paired up. The more shifts we worked together, the closer we became. Our post-shift bar crawls became a regular part of our routine. At a ratty bar off Front Street, Terry was outside under a green awning making a mysterious call on a pay phone, leaving me alone with Diane. It felt strange to be sitting there with his wife. I could tell they had been fighting again. They were delusional enough, stupid enough, immature enough to mistake their dynamic as romantic. But then again, I wasn't much better. I recognized a lot of Terry and Diane in my relationship with Carrie. It was a kind of crazy, unstable love of two toxic people colliding. It was hard to watch, made harder by the fact that it had begun to remind me of Carrie and me.

"Do you think we could talk?" Diane asked me.

It worried me to be alone with his wife. I knew how unpredictable, how violent Terry could get over her. God forbid he started to suspect something between us. And the closer I got to him, the more unstable he seemed.

"I don't think it's a good idea," I said. Diane struck me as the kind of woman who would lie to Terry and tell him I made a move on her just to see what his reaction would be. It was as if his violence was some sort of litmus test for their love. But she seemed to be bursting with a secret. She took another glance out the window to make sure Terry was still on the phone, then she started talking.

"Look, I'm fuckin' scared, all right. And I feel like you get it."

"Get what?"

"You're not like these other cops he's friends with. I feel like I can talk to you."

I adjusted myself in the booth.

"If someone sees us together and he gets the wrong idea, you're gonna get me killed. So whatever it is you have to tell me, save it. Or tell it to a priest."

But I knew I couldn't stop her from talking. So I took the recording device disguised as a pen out of my pocket and set it down on the table. I clicked it on. Whatever was eating her up inside, she had to get it out. And I needed to record it.

"I think Terry's in trouble," she blurted out. "I think he's gotten himself mixed up with some bad guys. Please, can we talk?"

"What kinda guys?"

"I dunno," she said. "He gets drunk some nights. Gets really sad. It's like this weird kinda depression my father used to have. He starts talking about killing himself. Like he's trapped with a secret."

When she said that, it felt like a gut punch. Thinking about suicide because of a secret that was eating away at you was something I could relate to. I knew how heavy secrets could be to carry and how they turned your body into a pressure chamber. In that moment, I felt for Terry, but I also had a job to do.

"What do you think he's got himself mixed up in?"

"I dunno, Aiden. But a couple weeks ago, I found a T-shirt in the wash covered in blood."

"Blood? Was it his shirt?"

She nodded.

"What do you think happened?"

"I don't even wanna think about it. I thought at first maybe he was selling drugs. But then one night, he gets so wasted and he tells me: I killed a guy. He gets so drunk I don't even know if he remembers telling me."

The portrait Diane painted of her husband was one of a violent alcoholic who got into contract killing to cover his gambling debts. Far as she could tell, he enjoyed abusing the badge and had no qualms with killing. A part of her was terrified that he would be arrested or, worse, killed in an act of violent retribution. But another part of her was scared for her own safety. How long until Terry's paranoia turned on her and she ended up dead herself?

"Look, these are some serious allegations you're making."

"I'm scared. You gotta help him. I don't wanna see him get hurt."

Before I could even answer, I saw Terry enter the bar, making his way toward our table. Without Diane noticing, I clicked the pen off and slipped it back into my pocket.

The truth took time. Building trust took time. With the recording of Diane, the police had enough to bring her in for questioning but I told them to wait. If they could get his wife to flip, it would go a long way toward bringing Terry down. But I was still missing the silver bullet: a recording of Terry admitting the murders. As powerful as her sworn testimony against her own husband would be, I was confident I could get Terry on tape. But I was rapidly running out of time. The agents were pressuring me to get the confession, and I needed to act fast.

One night soon after, we were cruising in a piece-of-shit Nova with our bellies full of pizza and beer. Terry drove us drunk from one bar to the next. We were at it again—drinking together after our shift, when I finally summoned the courage to ask him again about the murders, but this time I changed how I framed it.

"I've been thinking a lot about what you told me, a couple months back."

"What'd I say?"

"You know, about that guy Muller and all that."

Terry shot me a look and looked over his shoulder to make sure nobody was around. He looked as if he was surprised I knew—like maybe he'd blacked out his confession to me.

"What about it?"

"I was just thinking—you know, Carrie's been talking about starting a family. Moving into a bigger house. Life is expensive, you know?"

I needed him to think I was interested in getting in on the action. After all, it made sense given my past. I'd certainly seen my fair share of violence. It wasn't too far a stretch to think I'd want to make some extra scratch on the side. And Terry bought it. I could see from the get-go there was a certain pride he took in mentoring me about murder. He couldn't help himself. Just as he was about to start spilling his guts, I quietly clicked on the recording device pen and placed in on the bar. His eyes never left mine. I made my move.

"You don't gotta tell me."

"I remember you saying it could be a pretty lucrative thing. How much did you say you made?"

Terry looked around.

"Look, you wanna piece of the action, I'll connect you to the right people."

"I'm just curious how it would go. What was your experience like?"

Terry looked around again and took a big gulp of his beer.

"All right," he said. "Here's what happened . . . "

Without the slightest hint of self-awareness or doubt, Terry began to spill his guts directly into the recording device. In a voice low enough to be a whisper, he unknowingly admitted to murdering three different people for pay. In two of the incidents, he was the first officer on the scene. I left the bar that night with a stone-cold confession on tape. The following morning, I woke up early and drove back to Newark to hand deliver the recording to Agent Jackson. And for the first time since my life capsized nearly two years before, I felt as if I were part of something bigger than myself. I felt like I was making a difference.

Justice grinds along at a slow, methodical pace. Over the next few months, Terry and I continued our routine as squad partners while I waited for the DOJ to make their move. Every day with Terry was riddled with anxiety as I wondered every morning: Would today be the day he found out what I did? Then, on an otherwise ordinary Saturday morning, I received a phone call from a lieutenant at the precinct. The phone blared in my ear, shaking me from a deep sleep. Startled, I jumped from the mattress and groped around the side table in the dark for the phone. It was barely seven in the morning on my day off. I hit the phone with my hand and groggily said hello.

"Gabor?"

"Who's this?"

"Lieutenant Meyers."

"You need me to cover?"

"No. It's about your partner Terry. You hear?"

"No, what?"

My first thought was that he was dead, that his misdeeds had finally caught up with him and someone had taken him down. And as much as I had grown to dislike the guy, I didn't want to see him dead. But I did want him brought to justice. I braced myself for the news.

"He was arrested this morning. At his house. A whole bunch of FBI agents showed up at his house and led him out in cuffs."

"Arrested?" I said. "What the fuck for?"

"Apparently your buddy's had a lucrative side gig going on this whole time. He's been moonlighting as a contract killer."

I went quiet with disbelief. I couldn't believe it worked. I brought down a corrupt cop. But I had to be smart. I couldn't give the lieutenant, or anyone, any reason to believe I was an informant. I had to act surprised.

"The fuck did you just say?"

"Yup. It's all over the news. FBI raided his house this morning. Hauled him and his wife away in cuffs. The whole fuckin' precinct's been buzzing."

It didn't seem real.

"Jesus Christ," I said. "He woulda been the last guy I ever suspected of being a killer."

"You're telling me," he said with a laugh. "Sorry I had to be the one to tell you. I know how close you two were."

I thanked him and told him it would take a few days for it all to sink in.

"Gabor, before you go. He ever say anything to you about this? He ever mention any names?"

"No, nothing," I said. "He never said a word."

Terry's arrest got major coverage in the local papers. The town was talking. The precinct was buzzing. Every cop on the force had a different theory about Terry and what happened. The accepted line quickly became that he was sloppy, and the FBI popped him. Simple as that. But still there was a haunted, untrusting feeling in the air. And I could tell some of the cops—especially the cynical hire-ups—thought there was more to Terry getting busted than sloppiness. Rumors started swirling that there might be a mole on the inside. How long until they discovered it was me?

Anxiety defined my life. Worry wreaked its havoc. Taking down somebody like Terry has consequences that go far beyond one man. When you begin messing with the money of dangerous people, you become a target. Whoever Terry was working for was going to go looking for whoever helped bring him down. It could never get out that it was me. I started having nightmares. Waking up to the feeling of a cold gun pressed against the back of my head. The job started taking a toll I never expected.

My work snagging Terry got me kudos from the DOJ—and a small bonus—but the work was just getting started.

CHAPTER 6

T he kitchen phone blared, disrupting the quiet, piercing the calm. Couldn't've been later than six-thirty or seven. Morning light came filtering through the windows, dousing the house in cold, blue light. The phone continued wailing, waking the whole house up. Carrie groaned and covered her face with a pillow. The taste of blood was in my mouth from having chewed my cheeks all night. The dark dreams and nervous jitters of a man leading two lives.

I sat up in a groggy, half-asleep daze. Got out of bed, wrapped in a robe, and shuffled to the kitchen, where the phone kept screaming. Even before I picked it up, I knew who it was. Only one person called this early. It was Agent Jackson on the line, talking a million miles a minute before I even say hello. He was calling to tell me to meet him down near Station Four. There was a new target. A new name on the list and they needed me to help take them down.

Station Four was code for the Denny's off the turnpike out of town. We met there twice a month. Two hours east in a sleepy suburb called Montgomery. I dressed quickly in my uniform. Lied to Carrie and told her I had to work as I pulled on my pants and searched the table for my badge. It was an emergency, I said. The squad was shorthanded. But at this point, she was suspicious. I could tell from the way she just stood there with her hands on her hips that she was getting wise to my excuses. Did she think I was cheating? I couldn't be sure. But it wasn't another woman taking me away from her. It was a never-ending list of corrupt cops.

A cold autumn snap swept the city. I drove the quiet streets of the suburb, a couple hours north. The diner was nondescript. Far from the action. A depressing, twelve-booth joint that hadn't been renovated since it opened in the forties. The stink of spilled syrup wafted in the air. It was the type of place middle-class folks take their kids on a weekend to overspend on microwaved eggs and stale drip coffee. Still, I had my eye on the rearview the whole ride down. On the lookout for tails, wary of unmarked cars that might be other cops. My eyes peeled for anyone that might be on to me. The paranoia had officially begun.

When I finally got there, Jackson was seated in our usual booth, away from the bay windows so nobody could make us out. In those days, you could still smoke in diners in Jersey, and smoke mingled with the bacon grease stench. Jackson gestured for me to sit. He didn't waste any time getting down to business. What he was about to tell me would uproot my life for the next decade. He wanted to transfer me from Blue Bell—the small-town precinct I was at—into the Bluffs.

"Transfer?" I said. "It's only been a year. I'm doing good work. Just getting my sea legs."

In theory, he agreed, as he twisted his cig out in the glass tray and waved the waitress down for another cup. But Blue Bell was little more than a test run for me, a quiet precinct to see if I was some lousy insubordinate prick, some malcontent that would go rogue, or if I was someone they could trust. Turns out I did my job, and they got the message I was somebody they could work with. But they never had any intention of keeping me in the suburbs to help firemen get cats out of trees. They had bigger plans for me. And the bigger they got, the higher the risk became.

"There's just not enough action in Blue Bell," he said. "We got a tidal wave of corruption in your old neighborhood in the Bluffs. We need somebody on the inside. You did good on your first gig, and we feel like we can trust you. A little. So, we're gonna roll the dice and bring you up. It's your old stomping grounds. These are your people. If anyone knows the streets and the major players, it's you."

The logistics of a transfer like this were significant. The change would take months. I'd be forced to retake the officer's test. I'd have to find a precinct with an opening. And, hardest of all, I'd need to run it by Carrie and make sure she was cool with us moving again. It was a major life disruption, and I started to wonder if they even saw me as a human being, or was I just a disposable pawn in their game? When it came to employment, Jackson said he would try to grease the wheels but there were no guarantees. As I sat there contemplating what the upheaval would mean for my life, a couple things occurred to me. The first was that my best friend from childhood, Donnie Cooper, worked as a police officer at the precinct in the Bluffs. If I were to join, I'd have a good friend on the inside. Then something else occurred to me. I had a connection to the mayor of the Bluffs. His name was Paul Ciolino. He'd been involved in the Bluffs political scene since I was in grade school and had served as its mayor for years. In a town like the Bluffs everybody knows everybody. I had seen Ciolino stop by the garage a time or two, back when I was running with Eddy.

My eyes darted up to meet Jackson's.

"I think I might know somebody who can help us," I said. "Mayor Ciolino's a friend of mine."

"Yeah? You think he'd open some doors for you?"

"Only one way to find out."

A few days later, I took a trip home to the Bluffs. Monday morning, bleak winter cold. Downtown, the cold air flurried with bits of fluttering snow. The capitol buildings towered over the run-down rowhouses. A rush of suits in the courthouse square. Government workers, trial lawyers in square-cut suits. College kids milling about. The mayor's office wasn't as ornate as I would've thought. It was a drab, beige office building where Mayor Ciolino would hold pressers and host photo-ops. I had a nine-thirty appointment. Inside, I was met with a hush that reminded me of being in Sunday mass. The plush carpet and oil paintings on the wall made me feel as if I were in a library. I signed in with the secretary, told her my name, and sat patiently in the waiting room. A minute later Ciolino opened his office door to grab me.

"Aiden!" he said. "Look at you. Christ, how many years has it been?"

"More than a couple," I said, shaking his hand.

I followed him into his cramped office. He took a seat behind a sturdy oak desk scattered with books and paperwork. The walls were covered in black-and-white portraits of former mayors encased in gold-gilded frames. Ciolino took a seat and removed his glasses, cleaning the smudges with the tail of his coat.

"If you had told me five years ago that you of all people would be a cop, I woulda said you were full of shit. Look at you. The fuck happened? Last I heard you were heading out of state for college. Thought you were gonna play ball."

"Plans change," I said. "School was never my thing. I think I really found my calling doing this."

Ciolino nodded.

"Still talk to Eddy and the crew?' he asked.

"Not for years," I said. "You?"

"I see them around, but you know how it is. Guy in my position can't be seen talking to known criminals."

"Unless they become cops, right?"

Ciolino smiled. He had all the traits of a sociopath. He was glib and disarming. He exuded charisma, a smug kind of charm. He was your best buddy. He always had his hand on someone's shoulder. Always whispering into someone's ear. Look deeper, though, and you'd see a stone-cold absence in his eyes. I knew that look. I'd seen it in the mirror a thousand times.

"You know I'd love to spend all day shooting the shit," he said, "but I got a full plate, so why don't you tell me how I can help you."

I sat up straight and got to the point.

"Honestly," I said. "I'm working up there and it's not bad. Money's decent. Work's easy enough. But it's boring as hell up there."

"Not much action, right?"

"Not much at all."

As he began to catch my drift, he relaxed into his chair and crossed his legs.

"I miss home," I said. "These are my streets. These are my people."

"Bet you miss the old crew, too," he said.

Truth was, I did. And more importantly, in this moment, I wanted him to believe I wasn't some straight-shooting cop who was going to come and cause him problems. He needed to think I was the old Aiden from the streets. If he could trust I hadn't changed, he'd start feeling like he had one of Eddy Tocio's crew on the force, I might have a chance.

"Sure do," I said. "I just feel like I could get more done up here in the Bluffs."

"So we're talking about a transfer here?"

I nodded. "Think you can help me out?"

Ciolino leaned forward and dragged his hands over his face. He needed a minute to think.

"Here's the thing," he said. "We got a few slots open on the force. I can get you in, but you're gonna need to take the test again. Go through the whole process. But pass with flying colors and I'll make sure they take you on. How's that sound?"

To me, it sounded like Paul Ciolino was the head of a crime unit disguised as a police force. And he just unwittingly invited an informant onto his crew. I shook his hand and walked out. After that meeting, I only had one more hurdle to clear. Just before I took the police test for the Bluffs, I was called in by the police chief—a big, block-headed guy I'd known since I was a kid. His name was Chuck Lewandowski.

Lewandowski knew my background. I was a gangster, a criminal, and a car thief. I wasn't fooling anybody. He was suspicious of my reasons for wanting to join the precinct. So, on a quiet Monday afternoon, he called me into his office and told me to have a seat.

"Close the door," he said, gesturing to the empty chair in front of his desk. "I almost shit when I saw your name on the list of cadets. I heard you became a cop out in that little Podunk town in eastern Jersey. But it's a different world out here. This isn't getting cats out of trees. But I don't need to tell you about the Bluffs."

"No," I said. "You don't."

"It's just confusing to me. Why a kid who spent his entire life as a wannabe gangster would suddenly wanna become a cop in the Bluffs."

"People change."

"Do they?" He smiled to himself. "Listen, Aiden. I know you. I've known you since you were a kid running with Eddy Tocio. If you're gonna join the force, I need you to remember one thing: you need to learn how to toe the line. Can you do that for me?"

"Toe the line?" I said. "Sure, I don't see why not."

———————

After that, life was a state of perpetual upheaval. Moving boxes, storage units—my entire life stacked in the back of a U-Haul. We rented a small house in the Bluffs. Six hundred square feet with a tiny yard. We crammed the garage with taped-up boxes. Nothing about my life felt permanent. I felt like I was on the run, and in a lot of ways, I was.

The bureaucracy of switching police forces was a tedious bore. The next six months slipped by in a blur. I passed the city police test and Ciolino kept his promise. He pulled some strings to ensure my transfer and got me on the force. Weeks got swallowed up while I waited for the paperwork to be finalized. In the lull of nothingness— weeks lost sitting on my ass—my personal life changed forever. I decided to propose to Carrie. Things had gotten serious. The relationship was far from perfect, but at twenty-three, I was young enough, naïve enough to believe it'd get better. I thought we'd grow up and the fighting would calm down. At that point, my life was defined by disruption. With Carrie, even with all the volatility, I had the closest thing to stability I had ever known. She was a knockout who made me laugh, and when I looked at her I saw a chance to have a family of my own. She was an ER nurse and understood the pressures of frontline government service. She'd seen similar horrors that I'd seen. She was the first woman I had ever said the words "I love you" to. But I still couldn't bring myself to tell her what I was up to with the Department of Justice. It wasn't safe. But after two years of dating, I felt it was time to take that next step. I blew the bonus I got for bringing down Terry on a big stone from a Chinatown hustler hawking uncut diamonds.

By then I'd racked up enough PTO to take a much-needed vacation. Carrie's folks lived in Anchorage, so we skipped town for a week in late October. Flew coach to see her parents. In a lot of ways, the idea of proposing was scarier than bringing down fifty corrupt cops. The whole plane ride over, I was a bundle of nervous energy. Night sweats and dry mouth and restless, worried dreams.

The plane touched down in the dark afternoon. In the morning, still dark, after we settled in at her folks', I took a walk around the town. The lack of daylight was jarring, disorienting. The culture shock gave me a chuckle. The city was a far cry from Jersey. The pace was slower. People waving on the street. It had a good-natured, small-town vibe. The weather-beaten pickup trucks signaled a working-class town. The sky went on forever and the town was flanked by towering mountains the same way Jersey had towering skyscrapers. It was tempting to imagine a life out here. Witness protection. Change your name, change your life. Work a simple job as a cashier. I wondered if Carrie and I could ever be happy in a life like this, so far from the fast-paced world of Jersey's cops and criminals. Or was I becoming addicted to the hustle?

My relationship with Carrie's family was strained from the beginning. Whereas I was an only child, estranged from my father, she came from a large, tight-knit family—a sister and two brothers—and was heavily involved in their personal lives. This closeness made me feel secondary in her life. If there was one constant in my endless search for happiness, it was finding a sense of belonging in a family. And yet, this small, seemingly simple idea—belonging!—seemed to elude me. My own small family had been fractured. The family I found in Eddy and the DeCavalcante crew was a form of family, though being a Hungarian meant I would never truly belong. Football had elements of family, but that dream had been dashed long ago. So here I was, with no other options in sight, stepping into Carrie's family. But I didn't feel welcomed like a son or brother. I felt like an outsider, a spectator observing a family but never being invited in.

Still, we were cordial to each other. I got along well enough with her parents. And after a weeklong visit at their home (it felt more like a month and a half) Carrie and I reserved that last windless evening to go on a three-mile hike through a nearby forest reserve. At night, the skies over Anchorage were black, streaked with swirls of celestial, polar lights: blues and reds, golds and greens. After a few miles, I stopped walking. My hands were shaking as I turned and touched her shoulder and got down on one knee. She put her hands over her mouth when she saw the ring box in my hand.

Trembling, I asked her if she would be my wife. I wasn't ready. She wasn't ready. But she said yes. And on top of that mountain, we kissed and promised each other we'd be together forever. Until death do us part.

With the transfer complete and me settled into my new role as a beat cop in the Bluffs, news of my engagement to Carrie spread quickly. I told my mother over the phone. She feigned happiness for me but couldn't hide the quiet disappointment in her voice. She had always disliked Carrie and felt her motherly intuition should be enough for me to break it off with her. It always hurt her that I stayed with Carrie despite her urgings. I was too young, too enamored in love, to see what my mother saw. Soon after we made the announcement, the "Save the Date" invitations went out and Carrie's family threw together a gathering at the house of a family friend—an unofficial engagement party. When Carrie pulled up to the house, something about it looked familiar, though I couldn't quite name why. I felt as if I had been there before. It was a decent-sized place.

"This is Paul Ciolino's house," she said.

"Paul Ciolino?" I asked. "The mayor? How the fuck do you know Paul Ciolino?"

"He's family," she said.

Family? That corrupt piece of shit was family? It was in this surreal moment I realized just how close my professional life was getting to my family life. It's like I said before: in a town like the Bluffs everybody knows everybody. Priests, cops, gangsters, and politicians all intermingle. Turned out, Carrie's brother was married to Ciolino's daughter. It was a small world, indeed. And while Ciolino was something of a friend of mine, my time on the Bluffs force made it clear that he was just as dirty as any of the cops I was bringing down.

I was suddenly gripped with nerves I hadn't been expecting. If I married Carrie, my extended family would be linked to Ciolino. What did that mean for us as a couple as I dismantled his police force one cop at a time? In a way, the news of their closeness doomed me. While I had never told Carrie about my informant work, now I knew I never could.

The war was getting too close to home.

Inside, where her family was gathered, there was a buzz of celebration with an undercurrent of veiled hostility. I exchanged pleasantries with Carrie's parents, her brother Mitch, and Mitch's wife, Vanessa. Vanessa was the daughter of Paul Ciolino. On the table by the big bay window overlooking the yard, there was a spread of homemade food on the table. Heaping bowls of potato salad, fruit, sautéed chicken, and all kinds of desserts. Later in the backyard, I mingled with various pockets of her family, enduring bouts of tedious small talk, until I finally made eye contact with the mayor himself—Ciolino.

When Ciolino saw me, he did a double take, scrunched up his face as if he'd seen a ghost.

"Aiden?" he asked. "The hell you doing here?"

"I'm the guy engaged to Carrie," I said.

"No shit," he said. "You? I had no idea."

He seemed taken aback by the whole thing, before offering up a delayed "Congratulations."

While he pulled me in close and hugged me tight, I could smell his aftershave, the sting of his cheap cologne. He welcomed me to the family, patting me on the back like an uncle, but something felt tense and unnatural about it all. What did he know? Did he suspect I was an informant bringing down his police force? What did he know? Was he the mastermind behind all the corruption? How could a city have so many dirty cops without the mayor knowing? As I looked into his blackening eye, I knew something was wrong. Going back to our days with Eddy Tocio, I knew Ciolino was on the take. And now I would be forever linked to him through this marriage.

The party droned on. We drank too much. Sometime around ten, the family began to bicker. I knew it was time to leave. As we said our goodbyes, I saw Carrie speaking with Ciolino from the corner of my eye. Something about their closeness made me feel so utterly alone. On the cusp of our engagement, I realized a heartbreaking truth about my relationship with Carrie: I would never be able to trust her enough to share my darkest secret. Now, because of her bond with the city's corrupt mayor, I would be forced to carry this burden alone. I kept my eyes on Ciolino as I grabbed my coat from the closet. I watched as he hugged Carrie goodbye. She pecked him on the cheek. Then Carrie and I left together and didn't speak a word the entire ride home.

———————

Despite my mother's pleas for us to not be married, some things we just need to learn for ourselves. Even though Carrie and I were fighting a lot, it was too late to stop the marriage train. Besides, from watching my own parents, I just thought that that was the way marriage was.

Carrie and I finally got married a few months later. The ceremony was like a war zone, with each opposing side staking out its territory. One side was filled with officers, the other side with friends of Eddie. It was the first time I had seen my dad since the day I told him I was becoming an officer. We didn't have much to say to each other. Sam and Donnie, my two best friends from my childhood in the Bluffs, both stood with me as I took that step.

Sam, that geeky kid, had finally caught up to his big feet. He had grown over a foot since we first met. His braces were gone, and he had filled out just a bit. He was no longer the awkward kid I had met over a decade before. He even brought a date, a cute Hispanic girl who was about a foot and a half shorter than him. As much as Sam had grown, some things never change. He was still the smartest guy I knew and was still a bit of geek, even though I now had to look up at him.

Donnie was my best friend in the world. He and I had been through wars together and lived to tell about it. He was the kind of guy who would take a bullet for you.

Even though Donnie, Sammy, and I had been pals for over a decade, I still couldn't bring myself to tell them all my secrets. All they knew was that I had given up on my college football dream and was now a cop in the Bluffs. Neither of them knew about my days of running with Eddy.

Shortly after the wedding, I arrived back at Station Four to meet Jackson. He was sitting in the smoking section, somewhere near the back. The diner was crowded on a weekend morning. Now that I'd proved myself a worthy informant, I noticed he took a different tone with me. I had begun to feel less like I was his prisoner and even more like we were colleagues. I slid into the booth. We exchanged a few words of polite small talk. Then he slid a manila file across.

"Got another name for you."

I opened the file and inside was a report and a photograph. Jeff Walters, head of narcotics. But that was just his official title. Walters was suspected of trading inside information for the Vice Lords—one of the most dangerous heroin-dealing street gangs in America. The DOJ had tips that Walters was busting their rivals so they could run the drug corners unopposed in exchange for a cut of the profits.

"He's mixed up with some dangerous people," Jackson said. "Terry was just a warm-up. This is the big leagues now. The Vice Lords won't even bother to shoot you. They'll hack your body into a million pieces with a machete. You get made, you die. So you gotta stay sharp. Nobody can ever know you're an informant."

I looked one more time at the file and shrugged. "Let's bring him down."

Friday night blues. Rush hour hell. Gridlock on the freeway backed me up for miles. Red brake lights blinded the windshield. I sat in the grating blare of honking car horns and trapped ambulance sirens. Finally, after being stuck for an hour, I pulled my Bonneville off the ramp and drove around to the basketball courts. Any good cop has a network. A list of undisclosed informants that serve as your eyes and ears. I was on a mission to find an informant of my own.

I parked behind the courts. Streetlights lit them in a yellow glow. High-tops squeaked on the asphalt court as high school kids hustled back and forth playing a game of two-on-two. It was a rare day off and I was dressed as a civilian. In the distance, I could see the shape of a man sleeping on a park bench. A few steps closer and I could smell the reeking potpourri of dried piss, tobacco, and bottom-shelf booze. Most people would go a mile out of their way to avoid a guy like this. I was walking right toward him. The guy's name was Calian Chubbock. Junkie, drunkard, wastrel, thief. He lived off the res, thirty miles from home. In Jersey, he split his time between sleeping on park benches, passing out in ATM vestibules, and drunken, dizzy trips to the emergency room. As I got closer to him, I saw him stirring beneath a blanket made of newspaper pages. Something must've startled him, because a second later, he sat up and looked directly at me. He squinted his eyes. Wasted and heavy-lidded.

Couldn't tell if he was tanked or half-asleep. I'd known Chubbock since I was a kid but never knew him sober. It took a second for him to recognize me. When he did, he started to smile.

"Oh, shit, look who it is! Long time, no see, Cochise."

"Been too long," I said. "Thought you'd be in California by now. Living on the water."

"Nah, could never leave Jersey. Need to stay close to my mother."

"I heard your mother died."

"She did."

My informants in the Bluffs were hookers and addicts, street pimps and drunks. The dregs of society most people wouldn't dare talk to. But take a second to listen and you'll discover they know the city streets better than the police. Because they're invisible to society, they're able to see what others can't. To hear what others have ignored. I knew if I was going to bring down Jeff Walters and his group of narco kings, I was going to need help. That's where Chubbock came in. Chubbock had a rap sheet a mile long. A notorious bail jumper, he was always on the run from cops and judges. And a lifetime of boozing had left his brain in an unreliable fog. But he knew the streets better than anyone I had ever met. He knew the Latin Kings that ran the east side. He knew the Vice Lords in the south. He knew the cops that patrolled the streets. The Department of Justice had no use for a guy like Chubbock. Any halfway decent lawyer would dismantle his booze-soaked stories. Whatever testimonies he had to give would be inadmissible. But I decided his eyes would be my hidden camera on the back streets of Jersey.

Chubbock stood and stumbled. He was wielding a forty half-wrapped in brown paper. He took a swig and capped it.

"Heard you were running with the po-po now," he said. "Couldn't believe it. You becoming a cop after the shit you done?"

"Lotta guys switching sides as I understand it."

"Yeah, that's for sure."

When I first met Chubbock, he was hanging outside Eddy's garage with a bottle in his hand. Back then I thought he was just some funny drunk Eddy kept around to keep himself amused. Seemed a bit odd to me, though, why someone as wealthy and powerful as Eddy would keep some alcoholic around. As I got older, I started to think back to those days and suddenly it began to dawn on me. Chubbock wasn't a jester. He was Eddy's eyes on the street. He'd bring Eddy information and tips in exchange for booze and money. It was usually tips about cops. Now that I was on the side of the law, I needed him to do the same for me.

"Listen, I need your help."

"A cop needs my help? Never thought I'd see the day. You need some dirt on the corners out here? I can help you out if you can help me."

I nodded. "It's a bit more complicated than that," I said. "I got a bad feeling about one of my colleagues. He's pretty high up."

"No shit?"

"You know Jeff Walters?"

Chubbock started laughing. "Walters? The Narco King? Yeah, I seen him around. Why, what you heard?"

"Never mind what I heard. I wanna know what you've seen."

Chubbock scratched his scalp through his tangled, knotted hair. Took a swig of his malt liquor. Wiped his mouth with the back of his hand.

"I seen him on the corners with the Vice Lords. He's pretty buddy-buddy with some of those guys. Strange for a narco cop to be so cozy with a street gang."

Word on the street was Jeff Walters, the head of the narcotics division of the Bluffs police department, was acting as a double agent for the Vice Lords. The racket he was running was something of a perfect crime. See, the dope trade in the eighties was run by two rival gangs: the Vice Lords and the Latin Kings. It was Walters's job to oversee a special task force that oversaw the ports, monitored the corners, and cracked down on the importing and distribution of illegal contraband into the city. Instead, he struck a deal with the Vice Lords and was only performing busts on their rival, the Latin Kings.

That night, under the yellow lamps of the basketball courts, Chubbock said Walters and his boys would regularly bust the Latin King corner boys, confiscate their drugs, skim off the top, and split the score with the Vice Lords. Then they'd sell the rest. Walters had also been tipping off the Vice Lord bigwigs about major raids. All in all, he was pulling in thousands in stolen drug money on top of the dirty cash he was getting from the Vice Lords to serve as their informant.

The intel from Chubbock was a first step, but it wasn't a smoking gun. Chubbock's word would never hold up in court. I needed proof. I needed to see it for myself.

The plan was simple and likely to get me killed. I would wait outside the house of Jeff Walters and tail his car to see where it led me. It was stupid as hell, but I was going to do it anyway. I sat in the front seat of a borrowed red Camaro on the corner of Walters's block, just down the street from his house in the Bluffs. It was approaching sunset. The sky was darkening into night. I adjusted the rearview. Saw his one-story house. I waited. Waiting is part of the game when you're a cop. It often felt like that's all I was doing. Like a gargoyle perched on a high-rise in downtown Jersey, waiting and watching on high alert for something to happen. Most people think courage or strength is the biggest asset a cop can have, but it isn't. It's patience. A cop without patience is a dead one.

As I waited for Walters to show, I went over my alibi in my head. Sometime around five, just as dusk was setting over the suburbs, I saw some activity coming from his place. The back gate opened, and his clunky black Dodge came backing down the driveway. I relaxed the driver's seat, reclining down to keep myself out of view, and waited for his car to pass me. I waited a beat before starting my car. Walters's car drove by my periphery and my heart began to race. Showtime.

I rolled slowly behind him. Turnpike heading west. I kept my distance, four car lengths behind. My hands trembled on the wheel, and even though I didn't feel nervous, my body was betraying me with shaky hands and jittery knees. I couldn't pinpoint where the anxiety was brimming from, but I had an idea. I was scared. If I got made, I could get killed. And yet, somehow, I pushed on. At that point in my life, I still maintained a fearlessness, a bravado that bordered on worrying. Maybe, somewhere buried deep in a part of my inaccessible psyche, I felt as if I had nothing to live for. Logically I knew that couldn't be true. I had a mother that I loved dearly. I was recently engaged to a woman I thought I loved. Yet I couldn't shake the feeling that somehow this fearlessness was connected to a nihilistic pointlessness I felt toward life.

The low-speed chase went on for half an hour. I tailed Walters through the quiet suburb streets, the tree-lined residential enclaves of the Jersey suburbs, and onto the expressway, where I nearly lost him. Then, after spotting him again, I followed him into the suburbs of West Jersey, not far from the university, where the area slowly degraded, block by block, into a gangland.

I tailed him another few minutes until his car slowed in front of an alley. I slowed my roll and pulled up against a curb, about a football field's length away, and let the car idle. I pulled a pair of binoculars out of the glove box. I waited.

What the hell was this guy up to?

Then, out of the alleyway appeared two members of the Vice Lords gang. Walters rolled down his window. I couldn't hear what they were saying to each other, but I could tell by their body language it was friendly—too friendly for the leaders of a street gang and the Bluffs head of narcotics. From where I was sitting, a hundred or so yards back, peering through those binoculars, it looked like they were old friends, shooting the shit. Then, one of the Vice Lords started looking around, suspiciously, as if he were worried about undercovers. After a beat, he covertly handed Walters a fat envelope through the window. That was it, but it was enough for me to know Walters was on the take. A minute later, Walters put his car in drive and took off.

I should've just turned around and gone home, but I needed to know where this two-faced prick was headed with that package. I needed to know what was inside. Was it drug money? Was it dope? I needed to know, and more importantly, I needed proof. The DOJ would need more than my word; they'd need hard, physical evidence if they were going to take this guy down.

So, I followed him.

Forty minutes later, and Walters had unsuspectingly led me way out into some industrial area on the outskirts of the city. The rudderless roads were flanked by rusted fences topped with rolls of razor wire. Miles of dirt brown abandoned brick warehouses, oil-slick junkyards, auto part storefronts, repair garages, tire stores. The streets were pocked with potholes, and my car bumped shakily over the roads, causing my hands to nearly lose control of the wheel. What the hell was this guy up to? Whatever it was, it was shady, and I had to keep going. The windows of the warehouses were tinted black, many of them busted out. I was still far enough away that he wouldn't suspect I was tailing him. Still, as the roads become more remote and the streets more deserted, I knew I had to become more careful. We were no longer on the freeway with hundreds of cars to hide behind. Now it was just the two of us, and I couldn't risk getting made.

Somewhere down the road, Walters pulled into a warehouse lot. A few minutes later, I pulled alongside a nearby curb.

My tires went crunching over the gravel. Got close enough to watch him through my binoculars. Held my heavy foot down on the brake and watched him like a hawk. He got out of his car palming a yellow package. I watched him look around—the learned movements of a criminal—to make sure he was all alone. What was he so worried about? I wondered. In that moment, Walters didn't look like a cop or an innocent man. He looked like a desperate guy on the verge of something deeply, hor-rifically illegal. Then he disappeared into the warehouse. And that's where I lost him.

I knew I couldn't follow him inside, but as I took a look at the warehouse facade, something occurred to me: I knew that building. Back when I was stealing cars for Eddy, we would sometimes bring the stripped-down parts to these junkyards to sell them. I knew this warehouse and one of the guys who worked inside—an old friend of mine who ran with the Latin Kings. His name was Derek. Derek was the little brother of a guy I used to play high school football with. He'd been running with the Latin Kings for a couple years now. Thing was, the Kings had a blood feud with the Vice Lords, a corner war that had resulted in dozens on both sides being zipped up in body bags. I wondered if Derek knew what Walters was doing inside the warehouse where he worked. Was Derek in on it, too?

Or could Derek be my inside man?

By the end of the next week, I found myself back at the junkyard. The smell of oil slicks and burning rubber wafted through the air. It was late October. Cold and windy. Concrete paths of soggy leaves and puddles of rain. Broken glass cracked beneath my sneakers. I wasn't in uniform. Dressed like a civilian, I snuck right in and could've been anyone. I saw some guy, some grease monkey in a jumpsuit, carrying a car bat-tery walk past me. I asked him where I could find Derek and he jutted his head. Over there. And I followed the path of twisted metal and windshields and tires until I saw him. Derek was seventeen, eighteen. A good-sized kid. Arms inked up with gang emblems. He wore a long Eagles T-shirt and a pair of sagging Dickies. When he saw me from the corner of his eye, he did a double take.

"Aiden?"

I nodded.

"Shit, man. Been a minute."

We clasped our hands together.

"How's your brother been?" I asked.

"All good. Same old, you know how it is. Thought you were up in Michigan."

"Back home now," I said.

"Still running with Eddy?"

"Nope," I said. "Wearing the blue now."

"The blue?" he said, taking a step back as if I'd just slugged him in the sternum. "You a cop?"

"I am. Can you believe it?"

"Holy shit."

"Still the same guy," I said. "Just wearing a uniform now."

Derek paused for a minute and looked me over. "What brings you around here?"

"I might need a favor," I said. "Can we talk somewhere? In private?"

Derek must've seen in my eyes that it was serious. He nodded and gestured his head for me to follow him. A moment later, we were shut into a darkened room. No windows, no sunlight.

"A favor?" he asked. "A cop is asking a King for a favor. Okay, can't wait to hear this shit."

The sound of a whirring fan was all I could hear inside this sweltering garage where the two of us stood just close enough to make out each other's faces in the shadows and dark. I knew what I was about to ask him would set off the alarm bells inside of his head, but I needed someone on the inside if I was ever going to bring down Walters. With a jolt of sudden courage, I went for it.

"You ever see Jeff Walters around here?"

Derek paused. "Walters? The Narco King of Jersey? Yeah, I seen him. He pops in from time to time. Why, what do you know?"

I shrugged.

"I might not know anything," I said. "What do you know?"

Derek shrugged, too.

"Shit, I'm just an innocent bystander," he said.

I dragged my hands across my face. "Listen, Derek. You know me for how many years now? I ain't here to fuck with you. But I got it from a good source that Walters might be working with the Vice Lords. You heard anything?"

Derek squinted at me suspiciously. After a beat, he wiped his nose with his shirt sleeve and spoke.

"I can trust you?" he asked.

"You can."

"All right, listen. Word is, Walters's been on the take with the Vice Lords for some time now. This motherfucker's been busting the Kings, stealing our dope, skimming it for himself, and giving the rest to the Lords. He tips them off to raids. They got him in their pocket and ain't nobody can do shit because he's so protected. Nobody wants to kill a cop. It's fucked."

"What's he doing here?"

"He brings his stolen dope here to cut it. Repackage it. Been doing it for months."

It occurred to me in that moment that Walters must not have known that Derek worked at the auto garage. One of those strange, serendipitous happenstances that make real life so much stranger than fiction sometimes. All this time, Walters thought he was being so discreet, when in fact, he'd been bringing his drug scores into the den of the enemy. And his enemy happened to be a friend of mine.

"Look," I said. "I need your help. I need somebody on the inside here who can get me some proof. Photographs. Anything solid I can use that would hold up against this guy."

"You know who you're fucking with right now? This guy's got the Vice Lords behind him and the Bluffs cops. He's dirty as it gets, and if he finds out we're conspiring against him, we'll both end up dead."

"Nobody will ever find out you helped me. If he kills anybody, it's gonna be me."

Derek took a long breath and hesitated. I could tell he was conflicted about whether or not he should help me. Gangbangers like Derek get a reputation for being immune to fear. People mistakenly think they're not afraid to die. But many young kids in gangs are looking for family, community, a way to make a living. I knew that better than anyone. He didn't want to die. He was young and scared. But I needed his help.

After another long pause, he exhaled and nodded. "I have something you might wanna see," he said. "Follow me."

I followed Derek through the junkyard, into a back room of the warehouse I saw Walters disappear into a week before. The room was windowless. A stark, wide-open space with high ceilings and cement brick walls. In the center of the room was a large metal table.

"Take a look up there," Derek said, pointing to the corner. I squinted and saw something that looked like a light bulb covered in black glass.

"It's a security camera," he said. "Nobody knows it's in here. This is where Walters takes his shit when he comes out here. If you want, I can snag the security tape for you."

My mouth fell open. I felt like one of those Looney Tunes characters whose jaw would hit the ground. I couldn't believe what I was hearing. Video evidence of Walters unloading a dope stash would be enough for the DOJ to put this guy away. I had to get my hands on the tape.

"You get me that tape and I swear on my life Walters will never find out you helped me," I said. "In fact, you get me that tape, and I'll be sure Walters never fucks with you or your friends ever again. He'll be behind bars."

Derek nodded. He shook my hand.

―――――――

The very next day, I left work around five and drove thirty minutes to the warehouse to meet Derek. I wasn't expecting any trouble, but I had my gun in the glove box just in case. When I arrived, he was standing out front with the surveillance camera VHS tape in his hand.

"If anybody asks, we never spoke about this," he said. I agreed.

Back at home, with Carrie away at her sister's and the house to myself, I popped the tape into the VCR. The footage was black-and-white, grainy, but with a clear over-head shot of the metal table. I hit the fast-forward button and waited until I saw Walters appear. There he was, with three duffel bags. Unzipping them, unloading bags of stolen cocaine onto a table. Bag after bag of cocaine. He began cutting the dope and distributing it into smaller baggies before putting the bricks of dope back into the duffel bags. Then he started talking: "Ciolino's gonna shit when he sees the size of this score. The boss is gonna be happy."

It was the most damning evidence I could imagine. Jackpot. And best of all, it implicated the mayor of the city. I stopped the tape and sat back in my recliner with a smile plastered to my face. I had him.

The next day, I found myself back at the Denny's to hand the tape over to Agent Jackson. With each new score, Jackson became more comfortable working with me. More and more, I started to feel like a true colleague of his. But still I had to remind myself that I would never be like Jackson. Our relationship would always be transactional, and as much as I wanted to pretend otherwise, I had to force myself to remember that to a guy like Jackson, I was a mere tool. A pawn in his game. He was my friend as long as I was producing the goods. I had value. I had a purpose. But what was going to happen the minute he used me for everything I had? Where was I going to go after the last cop fell?

News of Walters's collapse broke fast. It hit the local news outlets and blazed through the neighborhood like a brushfire. The irony of the district's narcotics cop moonlighting as a dirty drug dealer was too much for the media to pass up. Still, I could feel our city become a bit more demoralized with each fallen officer. Each bust was a new betrayal. Who could you trust if you couldn't trust those who swear to protect you?

In the end, Walters was charged with aiding and abetting the Vice Lords on charges of extortion, racketeering, and intent to distribute drugs. Carrie watched the saga of Jeff Walters play out on the TV news over the next couple weeks. His mug shot seemed to always be on the nightly news.

Sitting there on the couch one morning, reading the paper together, Carrie blurted out, "I wonder how far up the corruption goes?" What would she say if I told her I was the one who helped bring Walters down? Would the truth of my double life bring us closer together? Would sharing my darkest secret draw her near or would it tear us apart forever?

———————————

A few months after Walters went down, two pieces of news changed my life forever. On an otherwise ordinary Wednesday afternoon, another major bust occurred. My friend and mentor Eddy Tocio was arrested in Portugal and extradited back to the United States. As a high-ranking capo for the DeCavalcante crew, Eddy's arrest hit the Bluffs hard. It was almost as if he was the godfather of our little town, and his disappearance left a void not just in me but in the city itself. For better or worse, Eddy was a pillar of the community, and when he fled from the government, we all felt his absence.

And now they'd finally caught him.

The news of Eddy's arrest gutted me. I was driving to work, zoning out to some morning talk radio news show, when the disc jockey mentioned in passing that Eddy Tocio had been nabbed and brought back to the States for a RICO trial. The news of Eddy's arrest spread even quicker than Walters's and dominated the news cycle for the next couple days. I was devastated. Eddy had been like a father to me, and in the absence of my father, his presence loomed greater than any other male figure ever had in my life. For better or worse, he was more responsible for the formative years of my life than any person alive. As the news of his arrest went pulsing through my shocked and saddened body, I pulled the car over and killed the engine. I took a big deep breath into my lungs. A moment later, the dangerous implications of his arrest began to dawn on me. For all these years, I had enjoyed a certain amount of protection because I was Eddy's boy. Nobody would dare touch me as long as Eddy was around. And even with him out of the picture, his influence still loomed like a shield. But now with him likely going to prison, that shield would no longer be there. If there were people who wanted me out of the picture, there'd be nothing stopping them now.

Then, a month later, another piece of news sent shock waves through me, forever altering the course of my life. After a double shift, I returned home to see Carrie standing in the living room in her nightgown with tears in her eyes. I immediately thought something was wrong. Had somebody died? Had somebody hurt her? I rushed to her to make sure she was all right.

"What's wrong?" I asked her. "Why are you crying?"

But they weren't tears of sadness; they were the tears of a woman on the verge of starting a family.

"Aiden," she said. "I'm pregnant."

CHAPTER 7

I woke up screaming with the cold sweats again. Gasping for air. Groping in the dark for my gun on the nightstand.

The nightmare went something like this: I was alone on a football field. Was it Jersey or Michigan? I couldn't be sure. Wandering under stadium lights. Then the power went out, and it was blackness for miles. Couldn't see, couldn't move. Couldn't see my hand in front of my face. Cut to the locker room, where it's cold and concrete with empty rows of steel cages. Someone—or *something*—was stalking behind me. I booked it down a barren alleyway. Then, in that way dreams can transport you in non-sensical ways, I was somehow a kid again, back in Eddy's garage. Still, I couldn't see. My arms were outstretched, blindly feeling my way through the dark. That's when I heard that sinister ratcheting sound of a gun loading. A chamber being cocked in a hand cannon. And that cold metal sting of a Glock, pressed hard against the back of my head.

That's when I'd wake up. Squirming, screaming. Three a.m. night panic. Basket case jitters. Checking my sheets for blood and bullet slugs. I'd sit up in bed on the edge of the mattress, feeling my brain stem for evidence of a gunshot. But I found nothing. Just evidence of my own paranoid subconscious. I clicked the lamp on. Light flooded the room. Carrie groaned and rolled away, sandwiched her face with the pillows to shield out the light.

"What the hell, Aiden," she said. "It's three in the goddamn morning. Do you have to with the light? Go back to bed." But I couldn't. My soul was scared awake. Teeth still chattering. I had sweat through the sheets so bad I thought it might be piss. I felt my face to make sure I was still here. And then it slowly dawned on me: it was just a dream. You're alive. For now.

After Walters went down, the nightmares began. Acid-trip dreams where I'd die in my sleep. Punishing night terrors so real I would wake with the taste of blood in my mouth. Nights on end, I'd scare myself awake. Grinding my teeth. I took the job home with me. I took the job into my dreams. I allowed it to consume me. I began to unravel. I started seeing things that weren't there. I was losing my fucking mind.

The next time I met Agent Jackson, he had a new assignment for me: the head of detectives—George Pellegrino. Pellegrino? The guy was a local hero. Heralded, revered. He was awarded the prestigious recognition of "Police Officer of the Year" from the bureau for a hostage situation he negotiated. He was a family man who saved lives. But there was another side to Pellegrino that only I knew.

I first met George Pellegrino back when I was running with Eddy Tocio and the DeCavalcante crew. George was only a beat cop back then. He'd swing by the garage after one of his shifts. And gamble with Eddy and the boys. He'd always leave with a package under his arm. I was too young then to know exactly who he was or what it meant, but I knew he was on the take. A dirty cop for hire. Over the years, it became common knowledge to most of our crew that George was involved in some illegal dealings—I didn't have specifics, just rumblings through the neighborhood. When he began to develop a reputation as a hero cop, the irony made me laugh. Only in the Bluffs could a corrupt cop like George be portrayed as such a saint. But everybody in the Bluffs had secrets. Like me, Pellegrino had been living something of a double life. He had the image of a hero with a murderer's soul.

Jackson sipped his coffee and explained. The DOJ thought Walters was just doing the bidding for Pellegrino. Walters was a fall guy. A flunky, a pawn. A spoke in the corrupt wheel of the Bluff's police system. He wasn't shrewd or smart enough to mastermind a con like this. Whoever concocted the deal with the Vice Lords was higher up. Walters was just some guy they used. He was a guy who needed fast, easy money that he could blow on coke and alimony, and they took advantage. But as he sat there across the booth from me on that diner off the highway, Jackson confirmed what I had always suspected. That this web was more tangled than any of us could ever imagine. The corruption in the Bluffs was like quicksand. And someday it would swallow me whole.

"What do you know about him?" Jackson asked, sipping his coffee.

I took a big swig of my tepid sink water and retreated into the corners of my mind where I had buried the incident. But it couldn't stay hidden any longer. And that's when my mind returned to a memory from five years back when I witnessed an execution that would haunt my dreams for years.

The Bluffs, 1990.

The main drag was cramped with bodegas and gun stores. I was still new to the force then, riding solo in my squad car, patrolling the beat, checking the corners for hookers and dope dealers. Sometime after lunch, a call came in fuzzy over the radio: a disruption at a convenience store off Elmwood Boulevard. Black male. Mid-thirties. Suspect potentially armed. I rolled my eyes and threw on my siren. Gunned it to the address. A few minutes later, I pulled into the parking lot. I was the first cop to arrive. But as I pulled my car in sideways, I saw something that didn't add up: the head of detectives, George Pellegrino, was already on the scene.

As head of detectives, George was one of the highest-ranking officers in the precinct's hierarchy. Why would a big shot like George be on a small-time call like this? This didn't require a detective, at least, not yet. Disruptions like these were often left to patrolmen like me, not higher-up detectives. So what was he doing here? At that time, I had only a few interactions with George. I knew his reputation as an expert detective better than I knew him. Still, I furrowed my brow and tried to make sense of it.

Besides my patrol car and George's silver unmarked, parked in a slant by the street, the lot was empty and littered with empty malt liquor bottles and crumpled packs of menthols. I strolled up to George and silenced my radio. He saw me but barely reacted, jutted out his chin as a way of saying hey. He was a big guy. Built like a linebacker. Broad shouldered and beer-bellied. He had me by a couple inches and at least forty pounds. That day, he was dressed in plain clothes and looking like he'd gone a couple days without a shave. He lit up a cig and ashed it onto the asphalt.

"What the hell are you doing here?" I asked him.

"Just happened to be in the area," he said.

I had no reason to doubt him.

"What do we got?" I asked him.

"Some junkie fuck causing problems. Typical ghetto shit."

"He armed?"

"Nah. Just disturbing the peace."

"We got a name?"

"Already ran it. Guy's got a rap sheet a mile long. Out on bail for a robbery charge."

From where I was standing, I could hear him: the belligerent rantings of a madman in the grip of drug-fueled psychosis. It was unclear what the perp was after. It didn't seem like he wanted to rob the place. Or kill anyone. Or even hurt anyone. Muffled by the window, he sounded just like any schizophrenic you might see on any street corner of an inner city. In my brief experience as a cop at that time, I knew he was more a danger to himself than to any customer. Our job was to deescalate and get him help.

Pellegrino agreed. He laid out the plan: he was going to go in first and try and talk the guy down. But he wanted me on alert for backup in case things escalated.

He drew his service weapon. I did the same. I radioed for backup, but Pellegrino shot it down. He didn't want to take any more units off the street. He thought we had enough manpower between the two of us to handle the situation. Truth be told, I was relieved Pellegrino was there. He had a history of successful deescalation missions, and I figured he would calm the perp down and we'd cuff him for disturbing the peace and call it a day.

Pellegrino ducked inside while I waited by the door that I kept propped open with my foot. The entrance chime dinged when he stepped inside. He moved through the aisles of potato chips and candy bars. Stood beside the cart of hot dogs being reheated under a low-grade heat lamp. The ranting became louder. The perp was toothless in a dirty tank top, jeans sagging down. When he finally noticed, he turned and began shouting at him as if he were some kind of demon.

"Who the fuck is this?!" he shouted. "No, you ain't taking me back!"

The perp leapt onto the top of a dairy freezer. He was screaming out prophecies about the end of the world.

"Come on down," Pellegrino said. "We gotta go. You can't be in here."

"Get away from me!" the perp yelled. He kept ranting and wailing until his lungs burned raspy. He looked wild-eyed. I could tell he was scared, like an animal backed into a corner.

"I'm gonna give you a five count to get down from there," Pellegrino said. "One, two . . ."

But before he even reached three, my eardrums ruptured with the sonic boom explosion of a firing gun. Everything went quiet. A piercing noise went keening in my ears. With the gun smoke wafting in the air and my hearing temporarily muffled, I felt dizzy, like I might lose my balance. What was happening? Was somebody shooting at me? I couldn't figure it. Then, as reality seeped back in and my focus resumed, I realized what had happened. The perp fell from the dairy freezer onto the aisle floor with a sickening thud.

Pellegrino had blown a hole in his chest.

I walked inside. Cautious, afraid of what I might see. There he was, on the floor with a dark purple bloodstain that was soaking through his tank top. He was still breathing. Gurgling. And then he stopped and died with his eyes open. Soon he was in a puddle of blood that went spilling out in a large shapeless river on the linoleum floor. I had seen dead bodies before, but I had always been able to justify it somehow. I told myself they were degenerates or criminals. I found some way to convince myself they deserved to die. Other times, I would rationalize it by reminding myself we were mobsters. We were expected to break the law. But this? This felt like I had just witnessed a murder. And what made it worse was that Pellegrino's job was to protect the public, not execute them. He had taken an oath to uphold the law, and here I had just witnessed him intentionally obliterate the law because killing gave him some kind of a rush. Pellegrino looked at me and smiled with the vacant expression of a sociopath. For him, it wasn't murder; it was target practice. He had them all fooled.

Sitting in the Denny's, I recounted the story to Jackson as I remembered it. He stared at me, unsure of what to make of the story. His blank stare worried me. Had he become so desensitized a cold-blooded murder wouldn't rattle him? I'd just confided in him that I had witnessed an on-duty officer execute an unarmed man, and he didn't so much as budge. He asked me what happened next. After the media hype died down around the shooting, an independent investigation ruled in Pellegrino's favor. They called it self-defense. No disciplinary action for Pellegrino. He retold the story a thousand times. He exaggerated his role. He made himself the victim and the hero. His fabricated story was soon accepted as truth. I was too young and inexperienced to step up and set him straight. I let it go. But I never saw him the same way again.

Jackson shrugged. "So?"

"So? I just told you I witnessed him kill somebody and you don't care?"

"It's a closed case. State's issue. Not my jurisdiction, not my problem. I feel for the guy's family, but that's not gonna help our RICO. I'm only interested in federal. I need to know how he's involved with the Vice Lords. I need you, Aiden. You think you can get close to him?"

I nodded. "Let me see what I can find."

———

Imagine a chessboard. Mayor Paul Ciolino is the queen. Beside him stands the king: the chief of police, Chuck Lewandowski. Like the king in chess, Lewandowski had a big title but was mostly a worthless, powerless pawn. On either side of the queen were two bishops: the head of detectives, George Pellegrino, and the head of the narcotics division, Jeff Walters.

Some days later, I began collecting intel. Parked my squad car on a drug corner of the Bluffs. Sidewalks tracked with shattered glass. Needles scattered in the gutters and grass. There I was, waiting with the window rolled down, taking in that sinister ghetto din of traffic and gunfire. Spats of broken English. Corner touts calling out drug orders in full view. It was a two-mile stretch of gun stores, liquor stores, twenty-four-hour bodegas, all surrounded by this open-air drug market that had the eerie tick of a time bomb. Nobody went there. It was too dangerous for tourists or locals. Most days, it was even too dangerous for the cops. It was the city's black market where fiends would limp and scurry along, begging dealers. I parked my car on the southwest corner and kept an eye out. Through a pair of binoculars, I saw him whistling on a stoop of boarded-up rowhouse. The guy I was looking for. This was Otis. He was sickly skinny, a hundred pounds and some change. Black, scabby skin with his front teeth missing. The faraway gaze of a man who's smoked his soul away. Crack cocaine was his disease, his mistress, his profession. Otis had a rap sheet a mile long. He'd been arrested dozens of times (some of them by me) for small-time intent charges. He'd spend a couple nights in jail. Do a month here and there in county lockup. Far as I could tell, he liked jail. And why not? Warm place to sleep and three square meals a day were better than sleeping on a piss-stained mattress in a crack den. For Otis, the slammer probably seemed like a vacation. But he always got out. Always ended up right back here on the street, slinging dope. It was hell, but it was familiar. I could relate to that.

I watched as he sat on his stoop with a forty by his feet, calling out to anyone who passed by who didn't seem like a cop.

"We got rock, we got rock. Forty for a gram."

I could hear from my car window, just out of sight. His drug-slinging cadence affected this singsongy quality, breathy, like he had a secret. Truth was, I wasn't here to bust some small-time dope dealer. Last thing I needed was more paperwork. Arresting Otis would keep me busy writing a report for two days. No, I had bigger plans. I had a feeling Otis had some intel stored away on George Pellegrino. Problem was, he'd never tell me. Far as I could tell, he hated cops. So I had to find another way in.

I watched him about an hour. Patient, focused. When it started getting dark, the market got buzzy with desperate, dead-eyed addicts. Otis started doing his thing, palming ounces of junk to his clientele, collecting small sums of cash he'd spend on crack or booze. He was trapped in a vicious cycle. But then I saw something strange coming down the street, and soon as I saw it, I got out of my car for a better look. Three clean-cut, preppy college kids came bounding down the street, straight off the bus. I knew exactly what this was. These mop-headed country club brats would take a detour to the city to spend their parents' money on some inner-city coke. I slipped through a break in a slat-wood fence and went quickly down an alley and out the other side so I could get a better look. I came out the other end, behind them now. They had that scared-shitless look of kids when they realize the drug underworld is not at all like what they've seen in the movies. But they also seemed suspicious, looking around for cops, not realizing they had one breathing down their necks. As I watched them approach Otis, I crouched down. As soon as I saw the coke trade hands, I'd make my move. Wait for it, I thought. Wait for it. The leader of the group, tall kid with an oxford shirt under a V-neck but with a sweatshirt hood over his head, did most of the talking. What they were saying was mostly inaudible, but I could read their body language. Otis was smiling at him. He wasn't a dangerous man, just a man forever trapped in the prison of his addiction, and he slipped a baggie of coke into their palms. The three boys started speed walking, down the stoop and right toward me.

"Police, don't move!" I shouted. Flashlight blaring in their shocked, terrified faces. I could see in their eyes they wanted to run. This could destroy their entire lives. "Don't even fuckin' think about running," I said. "On your knees, hands on your head."

Then, from the corner of my eye, I saw Otis watching me from the stoop. He knew me, though he couldn't remember my name. I wasn't sure he even remembered his own.

"You, c'mon," I said, waving him over.

"The fuck I do, pig? I ain't do shit."

"No, you gonna tell me you didn't just sell these boys some crack?"

"Crack? Fuck no. That shit'll kill you. These boys look like they smoke crack?"

Otis strutted up to me, fearless, close enough for me to smell his ammonia-tinged pipe breath. "I ain't got nothing to hide."

"No?" I forced him up against the patrol car. Hands on the roof. Patted him down. On the ground beside me, the three boys were trembling on their knees, hands glued to their heads.

"I see you toss something off the stoop there?"

"Me?" Otis said. "Nah, I didn't toss nothing."

"Stay right there, don't move."

I walked around the stoop and saw a plastic bag in the weeds. I picked it up and peeked inside. It was full of dime bags of coke. The perfect discovery for a possession and intent double charge.

"This belong to you, Otis?"

"Oh, that?" he said. "I don't know nothing about that."

"You're under arrest for intent to distribute contraband."

"Oh, fuck this," he said.

As I tried to cuff Otis, he resisted, wiggled, tried to squirm away, but my hand was clamped on his wrist. I wrestled him quickly to the sidewalk. It wasn't my intention to hurt him—not at all. I needed him. But I needed to get him alone. After I forced him into the back of the patrol car, I radioed for backup. Six minutes later, another squad car arrived. I relayed the story to the officer and handed over the three college kids to her. She would later book them all for intent to distribute narcotics.

I ducked into the front seat of my squad car, adjusted my rearview, and looked Otis dead in the eye. He didn't know it, sitting back there, but he was going to help me bring down George Pellegrino.

———————

Back at the station, the main floor was quiet. The brass was busy in a closed-door meeting. I led Otis to a small windowless room we used for storage. Uncuffed him. Bought him a Coke. Sat with my forearms on the metal, state-issued table and stared a hole into him. On the table beside me was a manila file stuffed with police reports.

"I ain't saying shit without a lawyer."

"What's your lawyer's name?"

"Like I'm gonna tell you."

"Where'd you get the dope?"

"I don't gotta tell you shit."

"No?"

"Nope."

I sat back in my chair and smiled.

"What if I told you that you weren't who I'm interested in? What if I said I needed your help?"

"My help? That'll be the day."

"Listen, Otis. You don't wanna go back in the slammer. And if I file this report, I'm gonna be up to my fuckin' elbows in paperwork. We both know how this ends. You go away for a couple months, then you're right back out on that street corner. Round and round we go. And the real criminals, the real drug dealers, they're still out there."

"Whatchu mean the real drug dealers? I'm the real deal, motherfucker."

"No," I said. "You're a puppet."

"Man, I ain't no fuckin' puppet."

"Yes, you are. And I need to know who's pulling your strings. I need to know who's out there calling the shots."

"Man, you sound like you been smoking some of this shit."

I opened the file on the table. "February 11 of this year, you're busted for selling thirteen ounces on the corner of Elmore. In the report you tell the officer you saw George Pellegrino earlier that day. You go on to say Pellegrino stole your drugs from you. Burst into your apartment without a warrant and ransacked your place. But then later, you walk your story back. You say it was all bullshit. I wanna know what happened."

Otis smiled a toothless, crooked grin at me.

"Man, who can remember that far back?"

I leaned in closer and tipped my hand, just a little. "Otis? If some cop is robbing drug dealers and redistributing that product to street gangs, I need to know. But I can't know unless you help me."

His face turned serious. A look of uncertainty, maybe fear, came over his face. I could feel the nervous energy radiating off his body. His breathing began to quicken.

"I just wanna make a living," he said. "I ain't bothering nobody."

"You're not the one I'm after," I said. "But if you don't tell me what you know, I'm gonna throw the book at you. With your list of priors, I could send you away for a long time. So what's it gonna be?"

"You a cocksucker, you know that?"

I shrugged and sat back in my chair.

"If I don't tell you, I go to jail. If I do tell you, they put one in my head and I go in the ground. What would you do?"

"Who's gonna hurt you?"

"I can't say shit. You putting a target on my back with this shit."

"Nobody is going to hurt you, Otis. Tell me what happened that night."

"You wanna see me dead?"

"No. I just want to know what happened."

"And what happens if I say. You gonna let me go?"

"You help me out, and I'll figure out a way to make this whole thing disappear."

Otis blew warm air into his hands. I could see he was trying to gather his thoughts. He paused and looked down at the table. His face was writhing as he tried to figure out what to do.

"All right, all right, look. Here's what happened. One night, I'm chilling at home, minding my own goddamn business, when that big ole white boy comes breaking down my door at two in the goddamn morning."

"What white boy?"

"Pellegrino. I was half-naked in my recliner, and this motherfucker comes barging in, grabbing me by my neck, and pushes me up against the wall. I said, 'The fuck is this? You better have a warrant.' But he ain't got shit. Tells me if I say another word, he'll kill me. He goes digging through my closet, under my mattress. Then he steals all my shit. About two months' worth of product. Just takes it like it belong to him. I paid good money for that shit, and he took it all."

"But he didn't arrest you?"

"No."

"Why not?"

Otis looked around, suddenly aware of what could happen to him if anyone found out what he was saying.

"It's okay," I said, trying my best to reassure him. "You can trust me."

"He'll kill me if he finds out I told you."

"Go ahead," I said. "Nobody's gonna find out."

In that moment, he looked as if he might shatter into pieces, his face regressing into a scared little boy. I had never been much for compassion or empathy, but in that moment, for the smallest second, I felt bad for the poor guy.

"He wanted the drugs for himself," he said. "That's what he'd do. He'd steal dope from us and sell it to the Vice Lords. Everybody on the street knows this racket, man. C'mon, you ain't no dummy. All these fuckin' do-gooder cops got their hands in the cookie jar."

I began to connect the dots in my head. On the surveillance video I saw of Walters, he referred to Mayor Ciolino. Ciolino appointed the police chief Chuck Lewandowski. Chuck assigned Pellegrino as head of detectives. It started to add up. It was a snake with so many heads. Pellegrino was running things on the ground. Ciolino and Lewandowski were pulling levers from behind the scenes. Walters had clout with the DEA and local narco cops. It was a tangled web of corruption that ran from the lowest rungs to the highest political vestiges of the Bluffs.

———————

Later that night, I called Carrie late to say I wouldn't be home for dinner. "Sorry, honey, they got me staying late again. I won't be done until the sun comes up. Yes, I'm being safe. All right, I love you too."

The clock on the wall read 11:57 p.m. The precinct started thinning out around ten. The overnights came straggling in, bleary-eyed and sluggish. Trudging into the locker room in their street clothes, lazily changing into their uniforms, talking shit and gossiping about the precinct. They'd see me on their way out, hunched over a typewriter. "Look at this guy. Shouldn't you be home? You got a pregnant wife at home. Burning the midnight oil, eh? Looking for a promotion?"

I'd give them the finger and shake my head no. "Finishing these reports," I said. And it was mostly the truth. Half-truths were a specialty of mine. The paperwork was endless. But I had a more urgent reason for being there this late, and my eyes couldn't keep from stealing glances at Pellegrino's office door, which was left open just enough to see the shadows escape. Around midnight, the office was a ghost town. In some far corner of the office, you could hear the grating peck of a typewriter. The gurgle of a coffee maker, the low-grade hum of a Coke machine. The fluorescent lights beat down on me as I finished the report. And when I felt as if I were alone, I made my move.

The door to his office was cracked, almost as if he were audaciously daring some-body to try to go inside. I pushed the door open and cringed as it creaked. I stepped inside where it was unlit and stunk of mildew. The desk a chaos of paper files, arrest reports, crime scene photos, affidavits, court records, and trial dockets. I didn't know what I was looking for, but I knew there might be something in this office that could give me an idea of what Pellegrino was up to. I was careful not to move too much of his stuff. I didn't want anyone getting suspicious. I stepped carefully, quietly, as I made my way around his office. On the wall was a plaque naming him police officer of the year. A framed photograph of his family.

Before this moment, I wouldn't have cared what happened to me. Blow my fucking head off for all I care. Death had never scared me. To the point I often wondered if there was something wrong with me. But now, with a son on the way, I had something to live for. It wasn't just about me anymore. It was both the sweetest gift and the cruelest twist: I was risking my life for my job when I needed to stay alive the most.

I snuck around the office for a few minutes longer, peeking through his papers, trying to find anything at all that could be incriminating. But I came up short. There was nothing. Pellegrino was shrewd and smart. If I was going to catch him, I'd have to be smarter.

———

Morning came with the usual nightmares. Panic that left me shaken. On my way to work, I stopped by the corner deli.

"The usual?" asked the clerk behind the counter, barely bothering to lift his eyes from the tabloid he was reading. I nodded. My usual: coffee, bagel, copy of the *Star-Ledger*. While I waited, I scanned the magazine racks, gazing at the newspaper headlines. In the blur of my periphery, I saw a tall black guy eyeing me from the other aisle. Didn't seem alarming, not at first, just unusual. I was armed and in uniform, but my mind flashed back to the convenience store murder with Pellegrino. Different store, different part of town, but still I made the connection. The guy stole another glance at me. I nodded at him.

"Order up!" the clerk said. I grabbed my bagel and Styrofoam cup of coffee and headed out the door. About halfway down the block, I heard some lead-footed steps clunking behind me. Coming up fast. As I got closer to my car, I could see him coming up behind me in the car window's reflection. It was the guy from the corner store. My mind began to race with possibilities of what this could be: Is he an associate of the Vice Lords, come to snuff me out? Did Pellegrino discover what I was up to? Or could it be a relative of the man Pellegrino killed in that convenience store, back for revenge? I set my coffee and bagel on the roof of the car and stayed calm. As he got closer, I quickly turned.

"The fuck you doin?" I said.

"Aiden Gabor?" he said. At this distance, barely a nose away from me, he didn't seem dangerous or even deranged. I looked into his eyes and could tell he wasn't going to hurt me.

"Who's asking?" I said.

He stuck out his hand with a note. "Be at this phone booth at five p.m. today," he said.

"What? Who the fuck are you?"

But he was already gone. Speed walking away, disappearing around the corner before I could say another word.

I opened the torn piece of paper in my hand. The handwriting was barely legible, but it had an address scribbled on it. I immediately knew what it was: the phone booth where I used to talk to Eddy Tocio. Eddy had been in jail a few months now awaiting his trial. It was something I tried not to think about. With every other part of my life on the cusp of collapse, I worked to push Eddy's inevitable demise out of my mind. But I knew it was coming—the day I'd learn that Eddy was going to prison, likely for the rest of his life. He would likely die in prison. And now, staring down at this note, it meant only one thing: the judgment day for Eddy Tocio was getting closer.

A few minutes before five, I took a break from my beat and drove to the pay phone. The gas station the booth looked out onto was dimly lit in toxic yellow light, just a few blocks from the garage where I used to hang with Eddy and his crew. While I waited for the call to come through, rain began to drizzle on the phone booth glass. Through the droplets pelting the booth, I was overcome with déjà vu and could imagine myself at sixteen years old, pulling into this station with Eddy and watching him from the car window while he took a call on this very phone. At that moment, it all felt like a million years ago. So many lifetimes had come and gone since then. And still, as I stood there in the booth, a part of me could still remember what it felt like to be that person.

A few minutes after five, the phone rang, scaring me out of a daydream. I answered on the third ring.

"Hello?"

At first it was static. Then I heard his familiar voice come through.

"Aiden?"

"Eddy."

"Jesus, kiddo. It's good to hear your voice."

He sounded older. He sounded tired. The tenor of his voice was still crisp and deep-throated, the way I remembered, but with the wavering quality of an aging gangster on his last legs. But exactly like I remembered. There was something comforting about hearing his voice. He had the same disarming tone that had been so critical to his rise through the family. He made everyone feel like they could talk to him. His voice was gravelly and distant, obscured by phone static on the line. I held the phone snugly in the crook of my neck. Rain slashed sideways, pelting the phone booth glass.

"Listen," he said. "I don't got much time and they're listening to every word so I need to make this quick. I heard what you were up to. And I just wanted to say I'm proud of you. You need to look after yourself. But I need you to do me a favor, kiddo. I need you to promise that you'll look after Little when I'm gone."

Little was his son.

"Keep doing what you're doing. You're making me proud. Never ever forget the family," he said. I nodded. "But remember, some people in the family might forget you. And you need to be ready for that."

These last cryptic words stung in my chest. *Some people in the family might forget you.*

"What does that mean, Eddy?"

"I gotta go," he said.

"No, wait, what does that mean? Hello? What does that mean?"

The phone went dead. I set the receiver up and stared off at the gray day, the traffic going by on the boulevard. I felt empty and even more lost than before. In a lot of ways, the call was like a glimpse into what my life would've been had I stayed with the crew. I'd be behind bars, rotting away in a cell, waiting for my trial, my entire life swallowed up by retrials and postponements and lawyer fees.

I stepped out of the phone booth and walked back to my car. Started it up and let my hands thaw out against the heater vent. All the while his words were on a loop in my head. *Some people in the family might forget you.*

What did it mean?

CHAPTER 8

After the call with Eddy, the nightmares got worse. I started waking up with numb hands and a low-grade ringing in my ears. Trembling on the edge of the bed, not sure what to say. There was one recurring nightmare that haunted me worse than all the others. I was being chased again. I couldn't tell who was behind me. Just shadows in the night. I was rushing away, hiding, checking side doors but they were all locked. And then, just as I felt I was in the clear, I turned and see a fire-scorched angel—Saint Michael, the patron saint of law enforcement—hovering over me like a judgment, like an omen, like a grudge. The angel held a sword, and as the blade got closer to me I'd wake up screaming, shivering from my paranoid dreams.

That's when I began drinking. Really drinking. It began to take over my life.

Truth was, I didn't want to live this double life any longer. I was worried about how deeply I'd delved into this sordid circle, and the farther I delved the closer I got to getting myself killed. The anxiety was eating me alive. Eddy had warned me there were only two endings for guys like us: prison or death. It seemed inevitable that his advice would be prophetic.

My descent into booze was slow and imperceptible. Sneaking drinks between shifts. A beer at dinner turned into three, four a night. I started filling water bottles and coffee mugs with gin and vodka. I'd fall asleep drunk with the TV on, cupful of gin, and quickly discovered that booze could drown my nightmares. Booze quickly became my best friend. Not since college, in those first days after I was busted by the DOJ, did I drink so much, so heavily, so recklessly. Booze was the numbing agent I'd been looking for. Only when I fell asleep drunk did I sleep through the night. I told myself I needed it to fall asleep. Then, after a few months, I needed it to get out of bed. I'd wake up groggy, stiff-jointed. Foggy-brained. Until I took that first sip of gin, then my mind would come awake.

Like all closet drunks, I became a pro at hiding the evidence. Pouring gin in 7-Up bottles and sneaking sips on the job. I hated the person who I had become. My eyes were perpetually bloodshot.

Those first couple months, while Carrie was pregnant, I drank to drown the pain. Drinking allowed me to forget the guilt of what I was doing. It helped me escape the reality that I was betraying the police force and lying to everyone I knew. The burden of being an informant seemed to disappear as soon as I'd get bombed. I learned quickly how to function drunk. I could work; I could act like a husband. To most, nothing had changed. But the people closest to me could tell something was wrong.

Some nights I'd get so wasted, I'd stumble home after a night at the bars and Carrie would smell it on me. She didn't marry a drunk. She couldn't understand where this sudden burst of self-medicating was coming from. And worst of all, I couldn't tell her. All I knew was that I felt better when I was wasted. I didn't feel like me anymore, and it was a relief to be rid of me.

My life quickly became trips to the liquor store. Hiding booze under the sinks. Soon, the drinking led to slower instincts. Making sloppy mistakes at work. Around this time, rumors started flying around the force that there was a rat on the inside. With Walters going down and my new task of finding Pellegrino, there were suspicions all around that somebody was leaking information to the feds. Everything was crashing at once. One night, I found myself at a bar near the house. Watching the Nets game. Downing my seventh beer. I remember a guy eyeing me from the end of the bar. Next thing I knew, I was being helped off the floor with blood pouring down my face, gushing from my nose. I came stumbling in that night with dried bloodstains on my shirt.

"The fuck happened to you?" Carrie asked. She was concerned, pissed, and disgusted all at once.

"Got into a fight."

"With who?"

I walked to the fridge and put a bag of frozen vegetables on my face.

"I don't remember."

"You need to get help," she shouted.

"Help? The fuck outta here. I'm fine."

"Fine? Aiden, look at you. You're not fine. You're an alcoholic."

There it was. The word I couldn't bring myself to utter. The word that was becoming harder to run from. I wanted to scream at her for even saying the word. But instead, I just walked to my room and went to sleep. I thought it was rock bottom, until a few days later, in a booze-induced fog, I tried to end it all. With no end in sight and no way out, I walked to the closet where I kept my .357 and a box of bullets. The alcohol helped to numb the nerves. I had never been one to consider suicide, but I couldn't take the burden I was living with any longer. Suicide felt like the only escape. After months of heavy drinking, I began to feel trapped by my addiction. The booze was a lie: it didn't erase my pain, it only deepened it. It depressed me, and the more dependent I became on it, the more trapped I felt. I was losing my mind, my health, and my marriage. If I kept drinking, I'd lose my job and likely my life.

I knelt on the floor of my bedroom and put one slug into the .357 and then put the barrel into my mouth. I spun the chamber and cocked it. Tears rolled down my face and my hands trembled. If I was meant to be in this world, I was daring God to prove it to me. I closed my eyes and bit the barrel. And with every ounce of fear and courage I had, I pulled the trigger. Nothing. The gun clicked but didn't fire. It was an empty chamber.

I fell to my side crying, curled up in the fetal position like a baby. I didn't want to be alive anymore, but I also didn't want to die. Lying there on the floor, I finally realized I needed help. A few hours later, after I cried myself to sleep on the floor, I pulled myself up and crawled to the kitchen. I grabbed the phone off the hook and dialed the number of my best friend, Donnie Cooper.

The next day, I met Don at a dead-end sports bar close to my house. There were regulars playing darts in the back. I sipped a cold one while I waited. My swollen red eyes were ringed with dark circles from sleep deprivation. I didn't know how I was going to tell him. I didn't know what I was going to say. But I was here ready to ask for help, and I thought that was as good a start as any. A few minutes later, Don came in, cold air trailing along inside with him. He was the kind of friend you could go months without speaking to and he'd still show up for you. With nobody left to turn to, I called him and said I needed to talk. He could tell from my voice it was urgent. As he slid out of his winter coat and draped in on the back of the bar chair, he said, "What's up, Aiden, your voice sounded shaky on the phone."

"Thanks for coming," I said. "I just haven't been feeling like myself lately."

"Work shit?"

I nodded.

"This fuckin' job, right? It's gonna kill us one day."

He said it jokingly, but he had no idea how right he might actually be.

"Listen," I said. "I ain't very good with small talk and shit like that. Truth is, I need to tell you something. It could get me fired. It could get me killed. But it's killing me to keep it inside."

"Shit, Aiden. What is it?"

The look on his face told me he was scared but trying to stay stoic for me.

"I don't think I know how to say it."

"What is it? You can tell me anything. You didn't . . . "

"What?" I said.

"You know? Kill anybody?"

I shook my head no.

"Then what is it?" he asked.

In that moment, I wanted more than anything to tell him. I wanted to say the words: I'm an informant. A double agent. I'm the one who took down Walters. I've been investigating Pellegrino. I'm the reason the precinct is crumbling. I wanted him to know I was the rat on the ship. But in that moment, I froze. Don knew Pellegrino. And even though our friendship was stronger than most brotherhoods, I wasn't sure I could even trust him. Maybe it was the booze, or the sleeplessness, or the paranoia, but I couldn't bring myself to say the words. I just couldn't. So I said the only other thing I could think of.

"I think I'm an alcoholic," I said. "I've been so fucking depressed lately. I can't sleep or function without a drink. My body's in so much pain. I just wanna die, Don."

"Hey, don't say that shit," he said.

"I'm sorry," I said. "But it's true. The other day, I took my .357 and . . . "

"Don't even fuckin' say it," he said. "Look at me. You ever feel that way again, you call me, okay?"

I could feel tears welling in my eyes. I was never much of a crier, but I couldn't hold my emotions in any longer. I felt as if this secret had been strangling me from the inside. Tears dripped down my cheeks and pooled in the crevice of my mouth.

"I know you've been through a lot," Don said, "but you got people out here who love you. You got a kid on the way. You have to stay alive for your child, Aiden. You can't let him grow up in a world without you."

Weeks passed. Sobriety didn't come overnight. It wasn't like in the movies when a guy gets a pep talk from his friend, and he's magically cured. I had the desire to be sober, but not the tool to get me there. Not yet. I'd go weeks without a drink, then I'd find myself unable to cope again. Anything could throw me off course: a fight with Carrie, a stressful workday, a vivid nightmare. I was too proud, too stubborn for AA, so I willed myself to stay clean and would push myself as far as I could, before stumbling back into the grip of addiction.

The investigation on Pellegrino had a similar trajectory. I knew I was going to have to tail him to see what he was up to. But Pellegrino was sharper, more skilled, and more deadly than Jeff Walters. He may have been a scumbag, but he was still one of the best detectives in the state, and if I made even one little mistake, he'd figure it out.

I was coming off a double when I got word. Sarge was waiting for me at the precinct with that scowl on his face. "Your wife's in labor," he said. "Our Lady of Lourdes Hospital."

Her family had rushed her to the hospital while I was working. I pulled up to Our Lady of Lourdes Hospital. Siren wailing. Speeding down the shoulder. Red, blue, red, blue. Lights from the ambulances spitting neon out into the night, the strobing lights pulsing off the hospital's facade, rotating in frantic spirals. My mind was pulled apart, unable to focus. I found a spot near the front and ditched my car in the lot. Hustled to the entranceway. Shouldered my way through the revolving glass door. Three in the morning and the place was a ghost town. At the information desk, a bored clerk read the paper while I rushed to her desk asking for my wife.

"I need to find my wife," I said. "She's just gone into labor. Carrie Gabor."

"That's Gabor with a G?" she asked.

"Yes."

Without a single ounce of urgency, she slowly checked the computer. I felt as if I might rip off my flesh waiting for her. Finally, after what felt like an eternity, she scribbled the room number down on a yellow Post-It. "Room 712B," she said, handing me the slip. "Maternity Ward. Take the elevators to seven."

I snatched the note from her hand and hauled ass to the brass elevators. Rushed my way through the white halls of the hospital. Gurneys clogged the hospital halls as I went desperately searching for Carrie. I squinted away the fluorescent white light that blinded me. The acrid stink of ammonia and bedpan piss sickened my stomach, made me feel queasy, weak in the knees and nauseous. The room numbers were going up

as I moved quickly through the maze of hallways searching for my wife. I was grabbing nurses, frantically asking where she was.

In every phase of my life, hospitals have been present. I was familiar with hospitals.
I'd been admitted overnight with broken hands from drunken fistfights. I'd sent too
many guys to the infirmary with cracked skulls. Carrie was a nurse, and I'd visit her
on her lunch breaks. But I'd never been inside a hospital on a day when life was being
born into the world.

"My wife is in labor," I shouted. "Carrie Gabor! Can somebody help me find her?"

But when I turned again, I saw my mother in the waiting room. I took a step back
as she stood to greet me with a smile. I hadn't seen her for more than a year. She
looked older, grayer than I remembered. But she still had this calming presence about
her that suddenly made me feel weightless. Seeing her now, I wanted to run to her,
wrap my arms around her, as if I were nothing but a mere baby, needing my mother's
embrace the same way my own child would soon be.

"Carrie called me," she said.

"I'm glad she did. Dad coming?"

"He's going to try and come."

At that point, I hadn't seen my father in years, ever since the night I told him I was
going to become a cop. And now, if he showed his face, he'd see me in my uniform.
I wondered if he'd be disgusted by what he saw or if he'd find it within himself to be
proud of me. I stood on the edge of fatherhood thinking of my own relationship with
my father. Was I capable of being a father? How could I bring a child into the world
when I lived every day on the precipice of being killed? Being a cop was dangerous
enough, but I couldn't shake this feeling that living this double life was somehow
going to end with me being killed. And then what? I'd leave behind an infant son who
never really knew me.

Inside the delivery room, Carrie was surrounded by a team of nurses. Her hair was
matted to her face, slick with sweat. Veins bulged in her forehead as she began pushing. I knelt down and she gripped my hand. The delivery took hours. I waited in the
room with Carrie and held her hand. After all the terrifying shit I'd gotten myself
into, nothing had me more scared than fatherhood.

Sometime in the middle of the night, as Carrie pushed through the final stages of
childbirth, I heard the cries of my son, Nolan, as the nurse took him into her hands.
They cut the umbilical cord. I felt something I'd never felt before. I felt love. I held

that baby in my arms and I felt nothing but pure, gushing love and devotion for this child I'd only known for only minutes. I was suddenly ready to be his shield and his protector, to do anything for him. In a split second, holding this pink baby, splattered with blood and birth, my life changed. And something else happened too. As I rocked my little baby in my arms, I began to wonder about my own father. I could never imagine throwing my own son out or going years without speaking. I could never imagine this innocent, perfect baby ever disappointing me. I wondered if he ever held me like this, if he ever felt this kind of love for me?

In the end, my father ended up showing up for the birth of my firstborn. He held his grandson in his arms. And even though I felt the rupture between us might never be healed, it brought me a certain measure of peace to know he was capable of showing his love for my son, if not for me.

The next day, I called Donnie Cooper. He answered on the third ring. I didn't jump right into it. We caught up. I told him about the birth of my son, and he congratulated me. We promised to make time to catch up. Then, as soon as the conversation hit its first lull, I went for it.

"Donnie, I need a favor."

"Again?"

"When have I ever asked you for anything?"

"You want a list?"

"I need to borrow a car."

"A car? For what?"

"None of your business."

"I think it's my business."

"I need to borrow a car, and you can't ask what it's for."

"What the fuck are you up to?"

"Can't say."

"Which car?"

"The Dodge."

"It's a piece of shit."

"I know. I might end up destroying it."

"You wanna borrow a car and you might destroy it but I can't know what it's for?"

"Exactly."

"Okay, come on over."

———

The red Corvette went peeling out, shredding rubber on the road, squealing away from the precinct's parking lot and swerving down the street. Pellegrino must've been doing ninety on a residential road, leaving a plume of black smoke in its wake. I quietly started Don's borrowed Dodge and began tailing him. At the supersonic speed he was flying at, I needed to be smart about the tail. Go too slow and I'd lose him. Go too fast and I risk getting pulled over. Pellegrino was hauling ass to the east side of the Bluffs. Binoculars on the seat beside me. I was flooring it just to keep the pace. Seventy, pushing eighty. I tailed him from a quarter mile back. Keeping pace. Losing him to the flow of traffic, but his red Corvette was hard to miss.

We were flying through the east side of the Bluffs. The entire neighborhood passed by in a blur: the liquor stores, the off-track betting shops. The schools and stores and garages where I used to hang as a kid. It all passed by outside the window. Pellegrino pulled off the exit. I followed close behind. I tailed him through the residential streets and into the gangland projects where the Vice Lords ruled. The deeper into their territory we got, the more certain I became Pellegrino was the one running the crime ring from inside the precinct. The most trusted cop on the force was moonlighting as a Vice Lord.

I pulled my car to a standstill and watched as Pellegrino got out of his red Corvette to meet some gangbangers on the corner. I stayed low in the car. Shaking hands. Embracing like old friends. Pocketing envelopes that I could only guess contained large sums of money or drugs. I'm not sure if it was the sound of my camera or just bad timing, but something near-fatal happened next: I made eye contact with Pellegrino as I took his photo. Oh shit, I thought. He just made me. Meeting eyes with Pellegrino was something like a death sentence. I needed to get out of Dodge. In the Dodge.

I panicked. I threw the camera into the backseat and leapt into the car. I revved the engine, threw it in reverse, spun around with a squeal, and hauled ass out of the neighborhood. I was gunning it. Odometer's pushing a hundred. Foot's gassing the pedal till the car is trembling and I feel like I'm about to rocket off the ground. I was bound to lose control of the car at any second, but my life was on the line, so I jammed my foot even harder on the pedal. Then, behind me, way back in the rearview, I saw a red Corvette, blasting toward me like a demon missile. I needed to outrun him. I couldn't let him catch me. If he caught me, I'd be dead.

I swerved. I zigzagged. I floored it down alleys, down residential roads. I took every shortcut I could find. Back on the New Jersey Turnpike, I thought I had lost him, but there he was, speeding up behind me. I couldn't shake him. He was relentless in his chase. He began speeding up now as I floored it to stay ahead. His car was faster, more horses, and I felt him bearing down on me. I was going to die. Any other time of my life I wouldn't have cared, but as I sped through the panic and fear, all I could think was this: I never got a chance to know my son.

And with that thought rattling around inside my head, I pushed on, even harder. I pulled off the exit ramp, hooked a wild U-turn, jumped the concrete median going the other way, and hooked around on the highway going the other direction, back toward the precinct. I floored it going northbound, and in my rearview, I saw nothing.

I exhaled a sigh of relief.

Somehow, I had done it. I lost him.

Hours later, back at the garage where the squad cars were parked, it was desolate and always seemed abandoned. I had heard from many of the women on the force how creepy it was to go down into our basement garage at night. Even with all their training and surrounded by so many officers, it still maintained this eerie, dangerous vibe to it.

I threw my car into park and rested my eyes for a spell. I was worried I might've gotten made. If Pellegrino saw me, that was it. I'd be finished. Possibly fired, more likely executed. These guys weren't fucking around. I started making my way through the dark garage. The stairwell from the garage to the offices was around back, and the surveillance camera that monitored the area always seemed to be broken. As I began to make my way up the steps, I felt an exhaustion coursing through my body. I didn't want to do this anymore. I kept thinking, I should be home with my family. I should be home with my son. I didn't want to be like my father, always working, always away. I wanted to be present. I wanted to always be there for my son. As I made my way through the garage, my state-issued boots made an echoless thud on the concrete. Right there in that garage, I made myself a promise: after I brought Pellegrino down, I would get out. This was it. This was my last rodeo.

I began to trudge up the long, dusky staircase when I saw the door open. The light from inside blinded me, and I saw only a large silhouette at first. Before I could even react, I saw this person barreling down the stairs toward me. It was Pellegrino. I tried to speak, but before I could mutter any words at all, I saw the mouth of a Glock pointed in my face. I closed my eyes. I tried to talk but I couldn't. I froze. Time slowed, and my mouth ran dry. And then he spoke.

"Why the fuck have you been following me?"

CHAPTER 9

I gaped into the face of death. I stared into the black eye of the barrel. There wasn't any time to see my life flash before my eyes. I'd heard it happens that way, but it doesn't. There was no moment of clarity. No flashbacks. No come-to-Jesus moment. Just the cold barrel of a Glock jammed into my forehead.

He stood over me. Three steps above. He looked ten feet tall, like an agent of death. With that bare single bulb behind him, he was half in silhouette. Backlit with orange light. His shadow swallowed me. He looked monstrous, hovering. The gun barrel was dragged down my face and grinded into my eye socket. I was paralyzed. I tried to suppress my trembling, but it was barely any use. If I made a move, I was dead. Reach for my gun, I was dead. Lunge for the door, I was dead. Blink the wrong way, I was dead.

And there wasn't a doubt in my mind that George Pellegrino had the audacity to shoot me right there in the stairwell of a police station. Shielded by a corrupt system, he felt more powerful than God. Untouchable. Him and his cronies murdered at will and knew they could write it off as "suicide by police officer." Just like with the homeless guy from the convenience store. He and I both knew he could get away with it. He could shoot me point-blank in the face and it would've been ruled a suicide: suicide by cop. He had no fear. That's how much power he had.

He pushed the barrel of the handgun against my temple, and I winced.

"I'm going to ask you again," he said. "Why the fuck were you following me?"

"I wasn't following you," I said.

"Lying to me now is a bad idea," he said.

On the cusp on certain death, I played the only card I had left in my hand: I bluffed. I filled my lungs with air and rage and decided if I was going to die there on that stairwell, I was going out defiant, loud, and crazy.

"Why the fuck would I be following you?"

I was shouting into the gun barrel as if it were a microphone. I wasn't going quietly.

"Tell me what you saw, you piece of shit, before I unload this chamber into your fucking skull."

"I didn't see shit. And what the fuck are you so worried about, George? Let me guess: you got some illegal side hustle going? Big fucking deal. You know who I am? You know who I used to run with? You think I give a fuck if you're making some extra scratch on the side? I was jacking cars when I was sixteen years old. I got a rap sheet so long it would make you choke. Whatever the fuck you're doing, I've done worse. Tenfold. So why do you care so much about my opinion?"

George stared me in the eye. I saw his intensity waver for just a second. If I could read his mind, I would've sworn he was impressed with my tenacity. Even with my life on the line, I was determined to be a prick to the end. Guys like George admired that. I wasn't sure if he'd buy the nonsense I just spouted, but all I needed was time.

"I knew you were a piece of shit since the day I met you," he said.

"You hate me because I know the truth about you. You're just a cog in the machine. I was part of a crew. And when you're a crew, you're in it for life. And that's what you wanted but never had. If you go down, they'll replace you in no time. I was the machine. You're nothing but a cog. If a machine breaks down, everything stops. But a cog? Cogs are replaceable. You're a wannabe. You're no different than a million other guys out there, wearing badges and trying make some extra money on the side."

He lowered the gun.

"I ain't gonna shit myself over some mobster pretending to be a cop. If I ever see you out there on the street again, we're gonna have a big fucking problem, understand?"

I nodded. "Next time you shove a gun in my face, you better be ready to pull the trigger. You understand?"

Pellegrino stared and squinted his eyes. I held the stare right back. Then, after a long, tense minute, he started laughing. Standing there in the stairwell, we shared this sadistic moment of sick fun, laughing about how close that tense moment came to utter oblivion. And then, rolling with this new sense of camaraderie, I asked, "So what's your game, George? I know you got your hands in some shit out there. I want in. Tell me what's up so I can get a little action."

"I'll let you know. Come on up. We'll talk."

———

I followed George down the precinct hallways. I knew he'd never be so brazen as to tell me about his illegal dealings, but I also knew I had him. I saw him interacting with the Vice Lords and that was enough to propel the DOJ into action. As I followed him into the station, the stench of stale coffee drifted in the air. The ceiling lights flickered yellow, buzzed like summer cicadas. From way down the hallway, George hollered that he'd catch up with me a bit later. We went our separate ways. Inside my chest thumped with the competing feelings of anger and terror. I was rattled from having a gun pointed in my face. My heart was still racing. One wrong move and my brains would've been splattered all over the stairwell. I was having trouble catching my breath and my hands were trembling with nervous energy. At the same time, I was fuming. The humiliation of being bullied like that was needling me, twisting in my ribs, and it took every ounce of willpower I had not to rip George's head off his shoulders. I wanted to kill him. I wanted to burn the entire police house down. These weren't heroes or idols. I wanted to release every ounce of furious rage I had. But I couldn't. I was so close to my goal: bringing them down.

———————

About an hour later, after I got my bearings, I was exiting the office when I ran into my best friend, Don, who happened to be coming around the corner holding a stack of police reports in his hand. He looked suspicious. His cop instincts had been triggered.

"Aiden, we need to talk," he said. "I just overheard some pretty unsettling stuff."

"What do you mean?"

Don explained that he overheard bits and pieces of a conversation through the door. According to Don, Pellegrino said he was "this close" to getting rid of me, but Lewandowski calmed him down by saying, "Aiden knows to toe the line. Don't worry about Aiden."

"What's going on with you guys? You in some kinda danger?"

"It's nothing," I said. "Long story."

"I got time," he said. "You wanna grab a beer?"

We left the precinct around nine. Arrived at the bar around nine-fifteen. Don drove. I rode shotgun but didn't talk. The entire ride there, I couldn't stop replaying the incident on the stairwell with George. I knew I'd be seeing that gun in my nightmares. It was the closest to death I had ever come. It had me rethinking everything. What was I doing? My life came so close to ending. All I wanted was to get home to my son.

After a couple hours of bullshitting and a friendly round of darts, Don finally asked me. "What's going on with you and George and those guys? You tainted?"

"Tainted? We're all tainted, Don. Look where we grew up."

"C'mon, man. You know what I mean."

"You've known me since we were in junior high," I said. "You know who I used to run with."

"Not really," he said.

So, I braced myself and exposed Don to a side of myself I rarely told people about: my days as an enforcer with Eddy Tocio and the DeCavalcante family. As I ran down my list of misdeeds, I saw Don's eyes widen with fear and fascination. I rehashed my youth with Eddy and all the illegal shit we'd done. There were some things I could never tell anyone, but for the first time ever, I let Don in on one of the biggest secrets of my life: I used to run with the mob.

"You motherfucker," he finally said when I finished. "You used to tell me you were caddying. Then you'd mysteriously have all this money. That whole time you were working for the mob."

I nodded.

"So what the fuck's all this shit with Ciolino and his guys?"

"That I can't tell you," I said.

"Aiden, c'mon. It's me. I'm your best friend."

I looked him dead in the eye. After all these years, I had never told anyone about my life as an informant. Not my mother, not my wife, not my priest. As I stared him in the eye, I realized this was the only time I'd ever be able to say it. I needed so desperately to unburden myself. He was my best friend. I had to tell him.

"These last couple years . . . " I said, my voice trailing off.

"Yeah?"

"I've been working as an informant for the Department of Justice."

"An informant?"

I nodded.

"They busted me a while back. When I was up at school. I had no choice, Don. It was either help them out or go to prison."

He had a serious, dumbfounded look on his face. I could tell he was trying to make sense of what was going on, but it was too unbelievable.

"All this shit you been seeing at the station. Walters going down. All that? It's because of me," I said.

"You're the rat on the inside."

"Shhh . . . keep your voice down."

Don dragged his hands over his face.

"Jesus Christ, Aiden. I had no idea. Why the fuck didn't you say something before?"

"How could I? I'm not supposed to tell anyone. They find out, and I'm dead. That's why I've been drinking. I had tried . . . "

But that's when the words stuck in my throat. I couldn't bear to say the words out loud.

My eyes fell to the floor, but Don lifted my chin and forced me to look into his eyes.

"Look at me," he said. "I love you. Like a brother. You made me a promise you would never try that shit ever again."

I nodded.

"No, I'm gonna need to hear you say it. Say the words."

"I promise," I said. "I have not since that night, but it's been hard. This double life. I feel like I am betraying my police family. We are not supposed to rat on each other."

"I know this is hard on you, man. It's gotta be killing you. But you have a reason to live now. You have Nolan. You have to stay alive for your kid. You got people in this world who love you. Okay?"

After the gun incident with Pellegrino in the stairwell, things cooled down. Because of my past as a criminal, they didn't suspect me. They knew me and the crew I used to run with. It must've seemed impossible to them that I'd be working undercover. In their minds, they had me under their thumb.

The diner stunk like ham steak and bacon grease. Mildewed carpets and torn leather booths. I ordered coffee but wanted a scotch. I shoveled a plate of burnt scrambled eggs into my mouth. My depression was worsening. My thoughts were getting darker. I needed to get out. I couldn't hold on much longer. The diner was like a prison. Two booths over, a white trash family was making a scene. I sipped my stale coffee and waited. The TV news was obsessed with OJ Simpson. Baseball was on strike. It was the nineties, and America was dying.

Jackson was late. Half past nine, he arrived with apologies. Slid in across from me. Ordered a coffee and lit up a menthol.

"What's so urgent?"

"I almost got made tailing Pellegrino," I said.

"So?"

"Fuck you. Maybe you wanna try your luck tailing a psychopath?"

"You wanna get smart? Or did you find something?"

"He shoved a gun in my face."

"You want a hug?"

"I want out."

"Doesn't work like that. You got something or not?"

"He admitted it to me."

"Who did?"

"All of 'em. Pellegrino. Ciolino. Lewandowski. The holy trinity of cocksuckers. They're all in bed together. Entangled with each other."

"They said this."

I nodded.

"I need proof."

"No. You asked me to get you some assurances. Well, here they are. I've seen them in action. You got video evidence. You got my word. You got informants corroborating. I can't take it any farther without getting myself killed. It's your turn to show up. I've pushed this shit as far as I can."

Jackson twisted out his cig. I could tell he was thinking.

"Where do they meet?"

"You know the park out by the junior college? There's a warehouse across the way that they've turned into a makeshift stash house."

I knew this by tailing Pellegrino a number of times. Just like Walters, he used this warehouse as a drop-off point. "If you can get inside there, you'll have all the evidence you'll ever need."

"We can't get in."

"Get a warrant. Bug their phones. Do whatever the fuck you gotta do. But it's them. I can't help you anymore. They're too suspicious. If they see me, they'll kill me. I've led you all the way to the edge, now you guys gotta close the deal."

Time passed slowly. I went back to work. Overnights and weekends. The justice system proved to be a sluggish chore. It took time, money, manpower. The system was rigged for villains. The system was as corrupt as the cops themselves. The reality of taking down dirty cops wasn't like in the movies. It didn't happen overnight. Justice was never clean or linear or sexy. It was bureaucratic. And after Pellegrino shoved a gun in my face, there was a low-grade tension in the precinct. But there was something else, too—an arrogance from Lewandowski and Pellegrino I couldn't have predicted. They felt they were so untouchable. And they had such little respect for me, they never feared me or questioned me after that. Their hubris had blinded them to what was so obvious: I was the informant all along.

It was a rush hour traffic jam. You had to be willing to grind. You had to be patient if you wanted to win.

At home, my son turned six months old. He had become my only reason to live. A little seventeen-pound ball of energy who had my mother's eyes and my father's smile. He would wrap his entire hand around my finger and try to make a fist. He was innocent. He was untouched by an evil world. I felt a new calling—to protect him at all costs. I knew, someday, I might even need to protect him from me.

My marriage was strained by my overworking and drinking. I would go months without a drink, but then the stresses of the job would overwhelm me, and I'd return to the bottle, desperate to numb the pain. The baby became a Band-Aid. Carrie started spending more time at her sister's. We drifted apart. Our conversations were all about the kid. We still loved each other but no longer seemed to like each other. We were living separate lives. I hid secrets from her. She hid secrets from me. Our marriage was complicated, often ebbing through flits of happy moments and then long bouts of silence and arguing. But still, we had a child together and stayed together for him.

On my recommendation, the feds bugged the offices of Pellegrino, Ciolino, and Lewandowski. They watched their houses. Held stakeouts outside their stash houses. They uncovered and dug into their shell companies. They found reams of evidence of wrongdoing. Money laundering. Racketeering. They had video and photos. Eyewitnesses. It took months. They filed petitions for warrants. They argued with judges. I marked the time with my firstborn's age. Soon he was eight months old. Then he was a year. I continued working as a beat cop. The feds continued digging. The one day, the hammer fell.

It was an overcast morning. I was home, in the kitchen, making my three-year-old, Nolan, some food when the phone rang. I let the machine get it. It was Don's voice. "Call me when you have a chance," he said. "It's urgent."

"The fuck could that be about?" I wondered. I set the food down and called him back. He answered out of breath. He didn't sound like himself. He was usually so composed. Mild mannered. Relaxed. But now he was shaken. There was panic in his voice. I knew what he was about to say even before he said it.

"You hear?"

"Hear? Hear what?"

"Fuckin' chaos at the station," he said. "The feds nabbed Ciolino, and Pellegrino, and Lewandowski. Pulled them out of bed and cuffed them on their front lawns. The whole town is buzzing."

Mayor Paul Ciolino and Police Chief Chuck Lewandowski were arrested and charged with racketeering, embezzlement, and conspiracy. The local news was full of images of them being arrested and led into the back of police cars. There was something satisfying about watching them go down but also something tragic. These were cops people came to depend on. They had breached the public's trust. The entire town was disillusioned. It didn't end there. It was never easy. Over the next couple months, they both posted bail and were free for a while.

Meanwhile, Carrie made it personal. She considered Paul Ciolino to be an uncle. She refused to believe he was as dirty as they said. She made Ciolino into a martyr and a victim. She questioned my involvement. She cornered me and asked me what I knew about the situation.

"What makes you think I know anything? I'm not involved."

"Bullshit," she said. "I know you're hiding something."

The arrests only added to our already frayed marriage. We were falling apart fast. She threatened divorce. She threatened to leave. I was ready for it to be over. But we had a three-year-old to think about, so we stayed and lied to ourselves that it would get better.

It took years for the dust to settle on the trials. But after a slow and vicious legal fight, Ciolino and Lewandowski both stood trial, and they both went down hard. Ciolino was sentenced to ten years for racketeering and money laundering. It came out at trial that he owned a telecommunications company two towns over that he was using to launder money. According to the judgment, Ciolino had to do at least eighty-five percent of his sentence. Lewandowski went down next. He got ten years, too. Pellegrino was the last guy to get arrested and sentenced. He was a slippery fuck who evaded the law as long as he possibly could. But in the end, justice won out. He got twenty-five to life for racketeering and conspiracy.

I sometimes wondered if they ever connected the dots. I wondered if they ever figured out it was me.

That should've been it. It should've been the end of my story. I should've ridden off into the sunset. And for a short time, it felt as if I had. I had a solid, well-paying job as a police officer. Carrie was pregnant again. Nine months later, we welcomed our second son into the world. For a short, sweet period of time, I had everything I had ever wanted.

But God had other plans for me.

CHAPTER 10

It was a cold, gray September. Then, the planes hit the towers and the whole world changed. Mine did, too. Agent Jackson called me up. Meet me at our usual place, he said. You ain't gonna like it. He was right. Turns out, they were moving me again. Out of the Bluffs to a small town across the state line in rural Pennsylvania. The news splattered me like a house being dropped from the sky.

The town was forty-five minutes from the Bluffs—a sleepy, conservative blue-collar hamlet of twenty thousand people where there was a large gaming casino and a giant, industrial prison. I'd heard of the town. Driven through it a time or two. It was a nowhere town where they bused inmates. It wasn't anywhere you'd want to live or work. All anyone knew about the town was that it revolved around a brick and steel prison complex.

"Why?" I asked. "What the fuck's out there?"

He nodded. He said there was a casino opening—the Embassy—and the guys running it were suspected of having mob ties. They needed an inside man. They needed someone they could trust. I didn't take it as a compliment.

Twelve years in, I had done my time. Over the years, my time as a police officer was strained by a conflicted, sometimes contradictory duality: there were times I actually loved being a police officer. The job was like an endless puzzle, and it required a certain fearlessness that I innately possessed. But the secretive informant work had frayed my psyche and my soul, leading my thoughts to the darkest corners of my mind. Still, there was a part of me that had grown to love police work, and I was surprisingly heartbroken to learn it would be coming to an end.

I had to leave the force, get hired as casino security, and be their eyes and ears on the inside. The news rattled me. I couldn't leave the force in the Bluffs. Not after everything I had been through. To Jackson, this was still a punishment. But to me, law enforcement had become my career, my identity. Being a police officer was the proudest accomplishment of my life, and now he wanted me to just abandon it and go become a security guard. And he said it so casually. I realized, in that moment, how little he cared about me as a human being. I had a wife and two young sons. I had a house with a mortgage. I had a career with a reputation. The Bluffs was my home. And what about the salaries? Would they be comparable? What about the health benefits for me and my family? But they hadn't considered any of that because they didn't think of me as a person. I was a pawn in their game. He didn't care about anything besides what I could do for them. And now he wanted to uproot me from everything I knew to go snoop around some casino. But when I explained this to Jackson, he didn't seem moved at all. Far as he was concerned, it was all part of the job.

I nodded. Toed the line. I countered with a compromise: I'll do the job, but I won't move my family. We'll continue to live in the Bluffs, and I'll commute every day—a forty-five-minute drive—to work at the casino.

Jackson agreed.

I exited the department without much fanfare. My work there was done. I decimated the district. I decapitated a four-headed snake. I made a checklist in my head. Head of narcotics, behind bars. Head of detectives, the police chief, and the mayor. All locked away. I exposed the corruption in the Bluffs and helped bring a measure of safety to the community I loved. The Department of Justice rewarded me by yanking me away from the life I had built and redistributing me to a dead-end town. I disappeared the same way I came in. I was the ghost of the precinct, and now it was time for me to go.

The small city in Pennsylvania. It was a quiet, dead-end Podunk town. It was only known because of the towering prison in the center of the city. The entire town seemed to gravitate around this brick and steel monolith. It was surrounded by a rusty barbed-wire fence, and the guard towers loomed above, high into the sky. The prison employed a good chunk of the city. I was on the outside, looking in. I didn't want to leave my position with the force. I had worked hard. I had started to feel, once again, like I belonged. But just as soon as I felt comfortable, it was time for me to go.

———

Three cataclysmic events defined the next few years of my life. The first was a death. It was a couple months after I'd left the force. I interviewed at the casino for a security job. They led me to a small windowless room. One of the hiring bosses ran down my resume. He thought I was overqualified. Asked me why I left the Bluffs PD.

"That's confidential," I said.

He asked me if I'd work midnights. I shrugged and said sure. They ran a background report. The DOJ had scrubbed my record clean. A few days later, I got the job.

The casino floors were choked with smoke. Locals blew their pensions at the slots. Chain-smoking grandmothers sat for hours at the crap tables squandering their Social Security checks. There was a depressing air wafting through the hallways. No windows, no clocks. A place designed for the desperate and destitute.

Five days a week, I'd make the long drive from the Bluffs to the casino. Carrie stayed home with the kids. The job paid well, but my heart wasn't in it. I kept a low profile. I slowly built trust with the casino owners. On weekend nights, when the bosses would bow out early, I'd sneak into their offices and snap photos with my Nokia flip phone. I took photographs of everything I could. Half the time, I wouldn't even know what I was looking at. But my job was to gather evidence and let the big shots sort it out.

I'd text the photos to Jackson. Then I'd go home and drink myself to sleep. I fell into a routine: work, drink, sleep. As much as I wanted to be sober, I couldn't lie to myself anymore: I was back to drinking full-time again. Hiding it from my family. Lying to myself. But my previous efforts to get sober had failed.

Then one night, everything changed. It was a weekend in the Bluffs. We went out for burgers. My oldest was peeking over the booth at the strangers next door.

"Nolan, knock it off," I said. My phone rang. It was Don Cooper. Carrie hated when I answered the phone at the dinner table. I answered anyway.

"What's going on, Donnie?"

"Hey, Aiden. Got a sec?"

His voice was somber. The shaken-up tone of a man still in shock. I could tell from the way he said my name that he was having a hard time getting the words out.

"Sure, I'm just at dinner with Carrie and the kids."

"Can you go outside?"

I furrowed my brow. "Yeah, why? Everything okay?"

"No," he said. "No, it's not."

I excused myself. Slid out of the booth. My oldest wanted to follow. I said, "No, kiddo. Daddy's gotta be by himself for a second."

I walked quickly out of the restaurant and into the cold Jersey air. Finally, he blurted it out.

Eddy Tocio died in jail.

My heart went quiet in my chest. I was frozen with shock. I swallowed slowly. Eyes fixed to the floor. I had been dreading this day since I was a teenager. I knew his health had been deteriorating. I knew the time on trial, in prison, had taken its toll. But I always held out hope that I'd be able to see him just one more time. I wasn't kidding myself: I knew exactly who Eddy was. But for all the harm he brought to the world, he gave me a place to call home when nobody else did.

After I hung up with Don, I took a moment to myself outside the restaurant. It was surreal, watching the headlights go by on the highway. The world just continued on as if nothing happened. My idol was gone, and time just kept ticking on. Relentless. Indifferent. Before I went back inside, I reminded myself of something. Despite every-thing that had happened with the Department of Justice, I never ratted out Eddy or any of the guys in his crew. I informed on corrupt cops. I helped take down bad actors on the police force. But I never turned my back on Eddy and his crew. And, in that moment, I felt a sense of pride of upholding my promise to never rat out my brothers.

Back inside, I slid into the booth. From the look on Carrie's face, I could tell my face look drained and colorless.

"Aiden? You all right?"

"Eddy . . . "

That's all I had to say, and she knew. "Oh, Jesus. I'm so sorry."

Carrie met me years after I stopped running with Eddy, but still she knew how heavy his presence loomed in my life. She slid out of her side of the booth and into mine. She hugged me. I rested my head on her shoulder and closed my eyes.

———

Shortly after Eddy died, the second bombshell dropped. Another sweltering summer passed, and an autumn cold snap quickly chilled the days. Leaves died on the branches. Gray skies came but never seemed to go. I'd been working at the casino for a couple years at this point. Come late October, I took some time off from work to attend a wedding in Las Vegas. The invitation was from an old childhood friend—Bobby V.—who was finally getting married. I wasn't a big fan of weddings—especially the weddings of straitlaced guys like Bobby—but I never missed a chance to visit Vegas. Things were slow at the casino, and I figured I could use an escape from the nagging East Coast bleakness.

Things were rocky again with Carrie, so she stayed home with the kids. I packed a small bag and flew west to Nevada with my mother as my date. Vegas held a special place in my family's heart. Over the years, my father had done a lot of business out that way, and we'd taken several trips together as a family, back when he and I were still talking. My mother was a gambler, my father was a hustler, and I was a product of them both. Something about the risk and desperation of the city felt so familiar to me. I was always drawn to places where outcasts went for one last chance at a happy ending. There was something sexy, romantic, thrilling about risking every single thing you had in the world on a single roll of the dice. It got my heart thumping. I was addicted to the rush of losing everything; and even more addicted to that surge of winning it all.

As usual, my father didn't join us. For the last fifteen years, my relationship with my dad had been strained, and it remained so, with each passing year only hardening us further against each other. But with so much time passing, my anger toward my father had faded. It wasn't the same white-hot fury I had once felt. Instead, it had dulled into a low-grade resentment. And sometimes, on quiet days when I'd be sitting in traffic on my way to work, it would strike me how much time had passed. I could see it as my children began to grow up. Nolan was already in third grade. Where had the time gone? We had lost so many years to pigheadedness. Two stubborn men, both refusing to blink first. There were times when I wanted to reach out and fix things between us—mostly because I saw how the long-term animosity was hurting my mother. I knew it was difficult for her to watch as her husband and son stayed locked in a stalemate of bitterness for so many years. And as my children got older, a part of me wanted them to know their grandfather. But each time I thought to reach out, something stopped me.

The trip to Vegas was uneventful, the wedding a pleasant affair. But after four days in the desert, we flew back to Jersey to a gut punch. The cab pulled to the front of the house. My mom looped her arm inside of mine as we walked up the driveway. She opened the front door and stopped after taking a few steps inside.

"Mom, what's wrong?" I said. I was following right behind her. When I walked inside, I saw what she saw. A half-empty house. It looked like someone had broken in and stolen half the furniture. But she and I both knew better. We hadn't been robbed—not in the traditional sense. But a theft had occurred. After more than four decades of marriage, my father decided to leave my mother without a word, without a note, without a sound. He waited for us to leave town, and in less than a week, moved his stuff out of the house and vanished like a ghost. He was too much of a coward to say goodbye.

That night, I held my mother in my arms as she fell apart. My mother was the toughest woman I had ever met. She was the only person alive who had the power to scare me. I wasn't afraid of a single man—no matter how big, no matter how violent. But I was scared of my mother. The things she'd seen and survived were beyond description. But losing my father that way crushed her and that night she wasn't scary—she was scared herself, at the thought of being alone, at the thought of being unworthy of a goodbye. I held her while she cried in my arms, and I quietly vowed to get back at him for what he did to her.

A few months later, I took some more sick leave and went down to Florida. I flew into the Tampa Bay airport and as the plane touched down on the tarmac, a wave of sadness washed over me. As a kid, I grew up dreaming of playing football for the Tampa Bay Buccaneers. How a kid from Jersey could love the Buccaneers was a mystery, even to me. Maybe it was the lack of a professional football team in Jersey. Or maybe it was that pirate logo. I always felt like a pirate myself, stealing people's gold, doing whatever I wanted. Or maybe it was some romanticized idea I had of becoming a big NFL star and making enough money someday to buy a mansion on the water. I had heard Eddy and the guys talk about Boca and Tampa, where they'd take their mistresses on vacation. For a long time, playing ball in Tampa was the biggest dream I could muster. I had never visited until now. And something about this first experience to the city left me remembering a time when I could still dream big. It left me melancholy and nostalgic for a simpler time.

Summer in Florida was choked with smog. The heat was a scorching ninety, humid from the tropical storms that had recently ravaged the shores. I found out through a cop friend that my father had ditched my mother to move in with a woman in Bradenton, Florida. I wasn't delusional about who my father was—I knew he was unfaithful to my mother. Always with some bimbo on the side. Those long Vegas trips where he'd come home stinking like another woman's perfume. But just like I stayed with Carrie for the sake of my children, my mother stayed with my father for my sake.

It was a sacrifice she made for me, for the illusion of family. But she knew and I knew that he was a cheater and a liar.

I didn't know how long he'd been seeing this new woman or how long he'd been planning to ghost my mother, but I was about to confront him. With the exception of my wedding, this would be the first time I'd see my father in nearly fifteen years and the first time I'd ever speak to him in any meaningful way.

I was only planning to stay a couple days in Bradenton. I stationed myself in a cheap motel and went to stake out the house where my father was staying. A few hours passed. I was using the skills I learned as an informant, tracking down corrupt cops, to track down my own father. When he finally exited the house, I followed his car over the Manatee River to a local bar on the main drag of Bradenton. I tailed him slow. I stayed low in the driver's seat. I parked around the back and waited fifteen minutes. Then I made my move. I walked into the bar on that weekday afternoon and saw regulars at the counter watching a low-stakes Marlins game. I told the hostess I was looking for an old friend. No sign of him. I peeked outside on the patio, and I saw him, sitting by himself with a cold one. There was nobody else on the patio besides my father. He looked tan, his skin browning and leathery. White wavy hair long, overgrown over his ears. A pair of sunglasses to keep the blinding midafternoon sun at bay.

"Dad?" When I called out to him, he turned. I walked quickly up to him and punched him in the face as hard as I could.

He spilled out of his chair onto the concrete ground.

"The fuck is going on, Aiden?"

"That was for Mom," I said. "For walking out on Mom, you prick. You weren't even man enough to tell her to her face? Couldn't even leave a note? Just walked out on her like a fuckin' coward. I should kill you."

"Just calm down," he said. "They'll call the cops they see us out here like this."

And just as he said that one of the bartenders stuck his head out. "Everything all right out here?"

"We're fine," I said, not taking my eyes off my father. "Just catching up with my dear ol' dad."

The bartender looked at my father for confirmation.

"I'm fine," he said. "Just fell outta my seat. We're all good."

The bartender went back inside.

"Can we talk?" he said. "You come out here swinging for no goddamn reason. You coulda killed me."

"I should've."

"Enough. You've always been such a goddamn hothead."

"I wonder where I got that from."

"I know where you got it from. And it wasn't from me."

"The fuck's that supposed to mean?"

I took a step backward while he pulled himself up and dusted himself off. He touched his jaw where I slugged him. It was already beginning to swell.

"Sit."

"I'll stand."

"Fine. I left because I felt I had no choice, Aiden. I love your mother. Always will. But there's things about her you don't know. I don't think we can get into it all here."

"What are you saying?" I took a seat beside my father. I could tell he had something on his mind. Something heavy that had been weighing on him.

"Your mom is a tough woman. She's been through a lot."

"I know."

"No, you don't. And she doesn't want you to know. Not while she's still alive. So outta respect to her, I'm not saying anything. But I left because I felt I had no other choice. I did what I had to do."

"And you couldn't have even said goodbye?"

"I couldn't, Aiden. Someday you'll understand."

And that was it. I got up from the table and left him there on the patio of the bar, with more questions swirling around my head than I started with.

———————

The third event happened a year later. I was finishing up one of my shifts at the casino when I received a call from my wife, Carrie, telling me that my mother had been in a car accident. My heart plummeted into my gut, but Carrie was quick to tell me she was alive and mostly unharmed. It was that goddamn three-way intersection she was always complaining about. She went through it without paying attention and got hit. Some kid sideswiped her. The front of the car took the brunt of it. But still, Carrie urged me to get home. My mother, at that time in her late seventies, was in the hospital as a precaution. The hospital only kept her overnight, but the family doctor, Dr.

Yelavarthi, decided to do an MRI. A couple days later, I went along with her back to the doctor to review the results of the MRI. My mother held my hand into Dr. Yelavarthi's office. Her arms and wrists and hands were bruised. Her body was sore and she was moving slower than I'd ever seen her. We sat together in Dr. Yelavarthi's dusky office on the fourth floor.

It had been many years since Dr. Yelavarthi saved my life after I was stabbed at sixteen. He was a longtime family friend and had been our doctor since we came to the Bluffs. He and I went way back to the days of Eddy Tocio. Dr. Yelavarthi was a regular at the garage. He would gamble some low-stakes poker with the boys. It would be incorrect to say he was a mob doctor or anything that sensational, but he was a doctor we could go to if we needed help without alerting the authorities.

And now I was back in his office, sitting beside my mother, waiting for the results of her MRI.

Dr. Yelevarthi removed his glasses and clasped his hands together. A solemn look came over his face. I began to feel a knot tightening in my stomach. He placed two X-rays on the table.

"Ms. Gabor, the MRI revealed you have a severe case of multiple myeloma." My mother looked at me confused. Scared. She looked back at the doctor. "Bone cancer," he said more bluntly. Then, with the tip of his pen, he showed us the polyps on her bones. On the X-ray, they looked like small black ants. Thousands of them. All over her bones.

At that point in my life, I'd been in knife fights, shoot-outs, car chases, and fist-fights. I'd been arrested and threatened with a lifetime in prison. But nothing was more terrifying to me than cancer—this invisible killer. And worst of all, it was happening to the most important person in my life.

On the drive home, we didn't speak. My mind raced with questions. Was God punishing my mother for my sins? I should be the one with cancer. Take me and leave her alone. She had never hurt a single soul. She never asked for a thing. If this was my punishment, it was crueler than any prison sentence.

My mother wanted to fight. Dr. Yelavarthi scheduled a blood transfusion. But the cancer was aggressive. It seemed to chew through her nerves and bones. I visited her every night after work. And every night she seemed to get thinner, weaker, older. She was deteriorating. The weight was melting off her. Hair thinned into graying wisps. I bought her a wig. We tried to keep up the appearance that everything was fine. But we couldn't deny the truth: my mother was dying. Her hands were skeletal. Eyes sunk back in her skull. I couldn't even bring my two young sons to see their grandmother because she was too scary to look at. I didn't know how to explain what was happening. I felt so responsible for her illness. I couldn't shake the idea that it was somehow a punishment for what I had done.

She was disappearing before my eyes.

———

The thought of losing my mother crushed me. It made me do things I thought I'd never do. A few days after the diagnosis, I picked up the phone and called my father. It had been years since I'd last seen him—and it felt like a lifetime since we had connected on any meaningful level. Our most recent interaction was violent, a hateful encounter. We were strangers to each other. I had spent most of my life trying to fill the absence he left. And when he abandoned my mother, I cut him off forever.

But in this dark moment of need, I felt he deserved to know that the woman he married—the woman he had loved for most of his life—was dying. Maybe he would prefer not to know. Or maybe he wouldn't care. But I felt he should know.

I dialed his number. On the first try, his new wife, Joan, told me he was out. I wasn't sure if she was lying or not. Was he avoiding me? Was he sitting right beside her, shaking his head, telling her to lie? I couldn't know. But a few hours later, he called me back.

"Aiden?" he said, his voice so familiar, even after an eternity. "It's your pop."

"Hey, Pop."

"Joan said you called. What's going on? Something the matter?"

"I'm not calling you because I want to," I said. "I'm calling because I feel I have to. Mom's not doing so well."

"What's wrong?"

"She's been diagnosed with cancer."

There was quiet on the other end. I had never known my father to be speechless. But we shared a moment of quiet as he searched for something to say.

"I'm sorry, Aiden. I feel so helpless."

As I recounted the story about how it all happened, I found us slipping into a conversation that was not about anger or complicated by our ugly history. It was about my mother and what we could do to make her comfortable in her final months.

I told him only what the doctors told me—that the cancer was very far advanced and the procedures she'd had done hadn't helped. The doctors gave her a matter of months to live.

I could hear the sorrow in his voice even as he tried to stay stoic. It didn't seem fair—the way our relationship had crumbled. Or the way he had just walked out on my mother, only to remarry a younger woman. It all seemed so cruel to me. And now, she was dying, and it was too late to make any of it right.

The call with my father was short. We didn't have much to say to each other. He said he would try and make it home from Florida to see her. He did eventually make it up, but by then she was too far gone to even know he was there.

On my son's twelfth birthday, it started to storm. The hospital called to tell me they felt my mother was on the verge of dying. I drove to the hospital with Carrie and the kids through sheets of sleeting rain. As rocky as our marriage had been, on that day, we were a family. Inside the hospital room, my mother was sleeping. She looked gaunt and shriveled in her bed. An IV threaded into her arm. A heart monitor beeping slowly, tracking her fading heartbeat. It broke my heart that people had to see her that way. All her life, my mother took such great pride in her appearance. She would've hated anyone seeing her that way.

As the storm raged on outside the hospital window, my mother started muttering to herself.

"They're coming," she said.

"Who's coming, Ma?"

"The Russians. Don't let them inside! Don't tell them we are Jews!"

I looked at my sons, confused.

"Ma, it's okay," I said. "Nobody's here. What Russians are you talking about?"

"They're gonna kill us all," she said. "We can't let them find us."

She was hallucinating. Her body was there with us, but her mind was somewhere else.

"What's she talking about, Dad?" my son Nolan asked.

"I don't know," I said.

I'd never heard my mother talk about Russians or being Jewish before. I knew she had been a young girl when the Russians invaded Budapest during World War II. But that's as far as my understanding went. I couldn't tell if her outbursts were the inane ramblings of a hallucinating woman on her deathbed or if they had some deeper significance.

She cried out for help. "They're coming to take me away!" she yelled. "They're coming for us all." Then she gasped, wide-eyed, and her breathing slowed.

My twelve-year-old, Nolan, took her hand. He talked to her and told stories and told her that we loved her. Slowly, the day faded into night and my mother held on for as long as she could. And then, sometime just after midnight, well beyond visiting hours, my mother took her last breath. She died surrounded by family.

Over the next few months, I spent my nights getting wasted at a local bar. The bar was called Joe's. It was a dive full of drunks and sad-sack locals. I went four times a week. Sometimes more. I'd spend half a paycheck downing shots of bourbon. Drowning my sadness, killing my liver. It was late. Eleven, maybe midnight. I was shutting the place down. Even as they were turning down the lights, I was there at the counter, ordering up another vodka rocks. I was alone with the weekend regulars, drinking myself into another life. Sometime around one, the bartender cut me off. "Why don't you go home and get some sleep, Aiden," she said. "Sleep it off. Tomorrow's another day."

She poured me one for the road. Put it on my tab.

I was lost and lonely and looking for a distraction. I was too drunk to think. I went stumbling out of the bar around two. The streets were dead. The whole town still and silent. Nothing stayed open past ten, except this one bar and an all-night diner. I went zigzagging down the block toward my car. The voice in my head was straining, begging me to call a cab. Nah, I thought. It's only a few blocks. I knew I was in no condition to drive. My inner voice reasoned with me: call a cab, Aiden. Don't do something stupid. But it was cold, and the booze was drowning my rational side. It was just a few blocks, after all. I could make it.

Standing in front of my car, I dug into my jean pockets and pulled out my keys. I clumsily dropped them on the street and went fumbling on the icy asphalt to find them. I stood up and lit a cigarette. I took a few hits. In the corner of my periphery, I saw a black car rolling toward me with the lights off. I took one more drag from my cigarette when the car rolled by. The window rolled down. And all I saw was a flash of white light and I felt the heat. I felt like someone was setting me on fire. But it wasn't that at all. It was a barrage of bullets hailing from the car window.

I hit the ground. The gunfire erupted all around me. I heard the whir of a bullet go zipping by my head. The rush of its velocity brushed my ear. The roar of gunfire punctured the quiet night. I felt its heat on my neck. And then, I heard the car stop. The patter of boots on the street. I crawled behind my car to the passenger side and heard the driver's-side window shatter into pieces. I turned to look. I couldn't see in the dark. I felt the heat of a dozen bullets come firing at me, riddling my car. Glass shattered. I covered my head as the bullets rained down and leapt over the hood of the car, landed on the ground, did a full one-eighty, landed with my head toward the front of the car, and looked under to see people running. I pulled out my P226 Sig.

I was drunk and dizzy but suddenly I was sober and alert. Bullets dented the car doors and blew out the tires.

How many shooters were there? Felt like two, maybe three. I heard voices and heavy footsteps on the street. I started shooting at feet. Aiming for ankles. I shot at anything I could see. I blew a hole in one of their calves and he went down in a heap. I saw one of my shots hit the shoe of a gunman and he went down hard, too. That was four rounds. I was keeping count in my head.

The gunfire only worsened from there. Shards of broken window glass erupted in fibers and showered down over my hair and onto my shoulders. I was bleeding—but from where? Was it my blood? Had I been hit? I couldn't tell. As they pumped my car full of bullet holes I made a move. I positioned my gun over the car hood and unloaded six rounds back at them. I was shooting at shadows, at phantoms, at ghosts. Who the fuck is trying to kill me?

I ducked. Kept myself hidden from the assault. Blood was leaking from my side and soaking through my shirt, spurting down my legs and pooling on the street below. I was losing consciousness.

I stood and saw a gunman coming toward me. I shot him in the shoulder, looked him dead in the eyes and put one in his head, right between his eyes. He crumpled to the ground. I fell down hard beside him. I didn't want to die on the street.

I was almost out of ammo.

My sons, I thought. What about my kids?

I had to keep fighting. How ironic, for a man who had spent so much time contemplating suicide, to suddenly be faced with death. But I didn't want to die. Every time

I closed my eyes, I saw darkness and this terrifying white that seemed to lull me into a false sense of security. I didn't want to go to sleep. I wanted to live.

With every fiber of my being, I screamed and stood and fired off another round. I felt a bullet explode into my leg and another in my sternum. I fired back and unloaded the clip. I fell to the ground.

I felt my heart slow in my chest. I saw my children's faces. And then I saw whiteness. I felt myself letting go. And then it all faded to black.

CHAPTER 11

Red blood, white lights. Blue moon. Darkness.

I woke up in a pool of red. Blood on my hands. Dozing away until I saw a light. The lull of Heaven. The voice of an angel calling me home. And then: panic. I swam away from the white light. Struggled to live. My eyes shot open. Pulse began to quicken. The quiet street was littered with broken glass and bullet slugs. My heartbeat slowed and thudded in my ears. Consciousness waned. Blood spilt from my stomach with every beat of my heart. I didn't feel pain. Just heat. I was dying in the streets. Bleeding out. One nine-millimeter bullet shattered my rib cage. Another was lodged in my spleen. I pulled myself into my car. My blood smeared on the car seats, the steering wheel. The windows, the dash. I had blood in my mouth. I fought to keep my eyes open, but it was fading. I saw my children's faces but even the love I had for my children couldn't stop the blood spilling from my side. I didn't hear any sirens. Nobody was coming to rescue me. I knew if I closed my eyes, I'd be dead within an hour. I pulled myself up to the car hood, leaving a smear of bloody handprints on the glass and door. Blood was everywhere. Shards of shattered windshield. The smell of smoke and burning flesh. As I stumbled, the sound of spent bullet shells went clinking around the street. How long was I out? I had no way of knowing. The gunfire had stopped.

I opened the passenger car door and pulled myself across to the driver side of the car.

The car went careening down the wet road. Veering into wrong way lanes. I was the only car on the road. I was behind the wheel, clothes drenched in blood, swerving down the side streets of the Bluffs. I kept losing consciousness but willed myself to stay awake. I had to get to Donnie's house. He only lived a few blocks from the bar, but I could hardly remember how to get there. I was losing too much blood to think straight.

I pulled up to Donnie's house. Parked crooked like a drunk on the street. His garage door was open. Before I got out of the car, I could hear his police dog, Dino, barking his raspy bark. I got out of the car and steadied myself on the car hood, streaking blood on anything I touched. I held my hand tightly over the gushing wound on my side and stumbled onto his grass and up his driveway toward the garage. Even though it was late, Donnie was still up, in the garage, getting in a nighttime workout. By now the adrenaline was beginning to wear off and pain began to rise throughout my body. Dino's barking got louder, and Donnie turned to look at me. I don't know if it was the shadows or the darkness or the blood, but he didn't seem to recognize me at first.

"Donnie," I said. I tried to scream but all I could muster was a whisper. "Donnie, I need help!"

His face turned white in horror.

"Aiden? What the fuck happened?"

I collapsed on the driveway. Donnie was a stocky guy, but he was strong as an ox. He hoisted me up. His face blanched when he felt my clothing sopping in blood.

"Jesus Christ, what happened?"

"They tried to kill me," I said.

"Who did?"

"I don't know."

He dragged me like packed meat to the garage. My heels dragged on the concrete. I collapsed again in a heap of lifeless limbs on the ground, my dark blood pooling and dripping into the drainage vents. "We need to get you to a hospital!" he yelled.

"No fuckin' hospitals!" I shot back. Growing up with Eddy, I'd heard too many horror stories about mobsters and gang members sneaking into hospitals to murder their enemies. Nothing would stop them. They were fearless and stupid and wouldn't hesitate for a minute to brazenly walk into a hospital and shoot somebody in the face if their boss told them to. Mobsters were mercenaries—like soldiers—and they'd carry out any order, no matter the risk. I used to be one of them. I knew the lengths they'd go to to see me dead. If I went into the hospital, I'd never make it out alive.

"No hospitals," I said again. Pain stabbed my lungs. I began to worry a bullet may have pierced my esophagus. I had no idea how many times I was hit.

"Well, we have to do something," he said. "I'm not gonna let you die in my garage."

"Call Yelavarthi," I said.

"What?"

"Dr. Yelavarthi!" I said again, this time through gritted teeth. "Tell him I've been shot. That I'm dying. Get him over here. He'll know what to do."

Donnie rushed inside to make the call while I writhed in pain on the concrete floor. I turned to take the pressure off my side. I was still losing blood. I thought about my children. Would I ever see them again? What would they think? What was the last thing I said to them? Had I been a good father? How would they remember me? All of these questions shot through my mind as I felt the pain pulsing throughout my body like a relentless electrical current. My body felt like it was on fire, as if someone had singed my shirt with a match and the flame swallowed me. I could smell blood, but worse, I could smell burning flesh.

I could hear Donnie arguing with his wife through the walls. She was screaming at him to get me out of their garage. "Take him to a goddamn hospital, Don! You want our kids to see this?"

But he just slammed the door and came rushing out into the garage with towels and water.

"Here," he said. "Yelevarthi's on his way. He'll be here in ten minutes. He said to keep your legs elevated and to stay hydrated."

He began moving the workout equipment around. Metal scraping the concrete floor. Dino's incessant barking was driving me insane. I began weaving in and out of consciousness. Spewing gibberish. Slurs of curses and vows of revenge and nonsense.

A few minutes later, Yelevarthi's car pulled up. Suddenly he was standing over me, shining a light in my eyes. He was an old man now, in his eighties, but at that moment, he was in a lot better shape than me.

"Aiden, you still with me?"

"I'm alive."

"First thing we need to do is get this shirt off you. I don't want you lifting your arms because I don't know where all the bullets are. Can you tell me where you were shot?"

"Not sure. Once in the side. Shoulder. Clavicle. About three, four times."

"Okay," he said. "Don't move. I'm going to cut the shirt off you and try to find the entry wounds to remove the bullets."

He pulled on a pair of rubber gloves and began cutting from the bottom of my shirt. Once the shirt was sliced open, he administered a shot that was supposed to help me manage the pain. It didn't take. Yelavarthi took out a small device that seemed to be a handheld metal detector. He began to run it over my body the way TSA agents do at airport security. He waved his wand over my arms and legs and midsection. Waved it near my rib cage. That's when the detector began beeping. Faster, faster. He held the device closer to get a more accurate read.

"Okay, I think we found one."

He wiped the gushing blood from my side and located the wound.

"This is going to hurt," he said.

"Just do it," I said.

From his medical kit, he selected a pair of surgical pliers. He sprayed his rag with disinfectant to wipe down my still bleeding side. It burned. It stung. Each time he wiped me down, more blood would spill out. Then he dug into my flesh with the pliers. I gritted my teeth. "Goddamn it!" I shouted.

The sharp edges of the pliers dug into my flesh as Yelavarthi went fishing for bullet slugs. I looked down to see the skin around each wound was singed. Burnt flesh from the heat of the bullet. He pulled bullets out of my side, my clavicle, my hip, and my stomach. He placed the slugs in a small plastic bowl. By now the anesthetics were taking hold and I was delirious with pain or drugs or both.

"Save me, doc," I said. "I have some revenge I need to get."

While Yelavarthi began stitching me up, Donnie was going back and forth from the kitchen to the garage with updates about the shooting. No witnesses, no police, he said. Nobody saw it and it looks like whoever was hit on the other side decided not to report it either. We had all elected to handle things the old-school way. It was a code among gangsters not to go to the authorities. We were keeping quiet.

The doctor threaded my wounds closed as I gritted my teeth to the pain. Every so often, he'd check my pulse, his fingers pressed to my thumping jugular or held to the underside of my wrist, to be sure my heart rate was steady. After two long hours of slow, excruciating extractions, Yelavarthi finally finished patching me. "Aiden, you are lucky to be alive," he said. "God must have other plans for you." At that moment, I didn't feel lucky. My whole body felt like a single lump of pain.

In the morning, I woke feeling as if I'd been hit by a bus. My entire body was searing with pain and soreness. Riddled with stiffness. I could barely move. I was trying my best to stay sober but all I wanted was a drink. I needed to call my wife and tell her where I was. I needed my children to know I was safe. But first, I just needed to get out of bed so I could take a piss.

Until that moment, I never knew how special it was to be able to stand up on your own. I suddenly felt guilty for taking so much of my health for granted. Eventually I stood. Bracing myself against the bureau and the wall. It hurt to wince. It hurt to breathe. It hurt to blink. I slowly shuffled out of Donnie's guest bedroom and into the bathroom across the hallway. Each step felt like someone was gutting me with a carving knife. It was the kind of shredding, relentless pain that makes your eyes water. I was short of breath. I hobbled into the bathroom and turned on the light. In the mirror, I looked like a zombie. Dead-eyed and pale. A white, bloodless face. I carefully lifted my nightshirt. My torso was bruised. Mustard-colored. Patched with cloudy yellow spots. Blotches of purple bruises. Burst blood vessels dotted my skin. It was terrifying to see myself so destroyed. My body ruined and ravaged by twisted bullet slugs. The gunfire decimated me. I knew I might feel pain with every step I took for the rest of my life. Some of the metal would live in me forever. Sure, I'd live, but I'd never be the same again.

Days passed. Donnie kept his eyes and ears open for news about the shooting, but no call ever came in. No news outlets got wind of it. It was something of a perfect crime—except I survived. I spent the next week at Donnie's house recuperating. Stewing. Boiling over with anger while I tried to figure out who the gunmen were. And worse: Who were the conspirators that tried to have me killed?

The list of people who might want me dead was long. I started with the guys I took down. It was a logical place to begin. George Pellegrino, Chuck Lewandowski, Paul Ciolino, Jeff Walters. Any of those guys could've heard about me being an informant. They could've put out some feelers on the street and paid to have me whacked. But this felt professional. It also felt familiar. The bullet slugs were from a .38 Colt. Most cops and their friends used Glocks. A Colt was a gangster's gun. And then I returned to that night. I was drunk. It was raining. Gunsmoke in the air. Bullets whirring past my head. I squinted as I got lost inside my mind's eye. It was hard to remember but one of the faces of the gunmen stuck out to me. Where had I seen his face before? It was a narrow face, with a bulbous nose. That's when it occurred to me: it was Freddy. Freddy was one of Dominik's boys.

Dominik—from the Bluffs. Eddy's lieutenant. The guy who gave me the nickname "Sandwich." Sat up on the couch. It was him. That motherfucker, I said out loud. It all started to make perfect sense to me. Of course, it was Dominik. He'd always wanted me dead. From the time I was a teenager and I hit him with a pipe. He vowed to me then he'd kill me someday. But this went beyond petty grievances. This was personal and business. He must've heard that I was a cop. He probably blamed me for the entire crew going down. Even from inside a prison cell, he put a hit out on me. All these years later, he was inside, simmering, growing more and more bitter, biding his time to take me out. I wondered if Ciolino or Pellegrino spoke with him. But it had to be Dominik. It just had to be. The only question left was: Why now?

As the days passed, I had nothing but time to think, to dwell on the fact that Dominik put a hit out on me. I stayed to myself in Donnie's basement. He'd bring me down some dinner. His dog, Dino, would come barreling down the stairs to play with me. Jump on me and cause me to shriek in pain. But otherwise, I was alone with my thoughts. At night, I'd listen to the tick of the clock and piece together a theory. What I finally came up with was this: Dominik and his boys thought I was the one who snitched on them to get them locked up. But for years, I had two shields, two layers of protection. I was a police officer, and I was Eddy's boy. They couldn't risk killing a cop. A cop hit could get them capital punishment. Or life in prison. And if anything happened to me, Eddy would retaliate. Even in prison, Eddy had friends. So they waited. They bided their time. Waited for Eddy to die. Waited for me to get released as an officer. On the day of the hit, I didn't belong anywhere. I wasn't a cop. I wasn't a criminal. I was just Aiden, a guy who worked security at a casino. And that's when they made their move.

My body healed slowly. My mind never would. Nothing vital was hit. Yelavarthi did a patch-up job. I'd live but I'd never be the same. I chose not to tell my wife or children. I didn't want my kids to worry about their dad being shot. They were too young. I wanted them to focus on school and sports and friends, not worry about whether their dad was going to be murdered. That wasn't anything for children to concern themselves with. But I couldn't hide it from Carrie for long. While we were still married, we had continued to drift apart. At this stage of our marriage, we were sleeping in separate beds and living separate lives. It wasn't uncommon for me to spend a few weeks at a friend's house or for Carrie to go to her sister's for a week and leave me with the kids. So, my absence wasn't much of a shock for the first week or so. When I finally called and told her what had happened, I did my best to minimize my injuries. I lied and told her it was a case of mistaken identity. I didn't want her to know any details. After all these years of marriage, I still had difficulty trusting her. She went quiet on the other end of the phone. Facing death made me want something with Carrie I hadn't wanted for a long time—I wanted us both to be happy. I wasn't sure if that meant together or apart, but all our fighting seemed so petty as I lay in the street. As her silence grew on the other end of the phone, I thought she might be thinking the same thing.

"Jesus Christ, Aiden," she said. "Thank God you're alive."

"I'm gonna stay at Donnie's for a little while longer," I said. "I wanna heal before I come home. I don't want the kids to see me like this. I don't want them to worry. Please don't tell them."

"I won't," she said.

"I'll talk to you soon."

"Aiden?" she said before I hung up. "I love you."

I think that might've been the last time she ever said it.

———————

All I wanted was to see my children. By this point, Nolan and Christopher were twelve and ten. Christopher had recently been diagnosed with special needs. He was on the autism spectrum. They were the reason I fought to stay alive. I didn't want them to see me in pain, but I couldn't disappear from their lives. I had to grit my teeth. Pretend I was fine. Two weeks after the shooting, the pain was beginning to wane. I could stand on my own without a cane. I could shuffle to the bathroom without too much agony. I could sleep through the night without waking up screaming.

I made plans with Carrie to drop the kids by Donnie's place. Donnie was their godfather. Carrie dropped the kids off. She stayed close by the car while the kids came running up the front lawn to greet me. I wore long sleeves and long pants to hide any evidence of the gunshots.

"Heya, kiddos!" I said as they rushed up to hug me. I winced when Chris wrapped his twiglike arms around my waist. Even the gentlest hug from the gentlest boy felt like a baseball bat to the ribs.

"What happened to your face?" Nolan asked, immediately noticing the bruises.

"Oh, your dad's a klutz and fell off a ladder while helping Uncle Donnie paint his garage."

"You fell?"

I looked up at Carrie, who was standing there with her arms crossed, shaking her head.

"Yeah, but don't worry," I said. "Your dad's a tough guy. It'll be healed up in no time."

I took my kids to the movies. Chris sat up front, Nolan in the back. They were horsing around, antagonizing each other as brothers do.

"Dad, Nolan won't stop kicking the seat," Chris said.

"Nolan, knock it off."

"Dad," Chris said again. "He won't quit!"

I smirked. Truth was, it brought me a small sense of joy to hear them teasing each other. I never had a brother myself. I grew up lonely, searching for boys who could be my brother, for men who could replace my father. I had been trying to glue together a family from broken pieces for as long as I could remember. And now, as a father, hearing my children bickering brought me a sense of joy. Because I was alive to hear it. Before the shooting, the smallest things would irritate me. All their annoying, grating fights and arguments seemed like constant obstacles to overcome—until I almost died. Then suddenly, the sounds of my kids fighting couldn't help but make me smile.

"Dad, ever hear of a Hertz doughnut?" Nolan asked me, snapping me out of my daydream.

"No."

He reared back and slugged me in the arm, not far from one of the most serious bruises. I nearly swerved off the road it hurt so badly. There's no way he could've known. But still the sharp pain struck through my body. I grimaced and gritted my teeth.

The next morning, I puked black bile in a bedside pot. It was part of healing from a gunshot. Three weeks later and my flesh was still burning. Each step up the stairs elicited a wince and a whimper. It felt as if someone were stabbing me in the sternum. A crowbar prying my ribs apart. I palmed three painkillers with a glass of sink water. I made it up the stairs and asked Donnie for a favor. I needed him to drive me out by Newark to meet Agent Jackson. I knew they would eventually find out about the shooting. I needed to talk to them and tell them what happened.

Everything hurt. Breathing hurt. Laughing hurt. I hobbled outside and ducked into the car like I was ninety years old. Slow and pained. I could barely move.

Donnie drove me out to the diner where I usually met the agents. My relationship with Agent Jackson had fallen into the background since I'd been moved out of the Bluffs. Our meetings began to wane. In the beginning, we met every week. Constant communication. As the bodies began to fall, our meeting frequency ratcheted up. But once I left the Bluffs PD, my role was diminished and our meetings lessened. We started meeting quarterly, and then, for the last couple years, once or twice a year. I was being phased out. They got what they needed from me and now I was just a worthless appendage to them. What was my value?

Donnie dropped me outside the Denny's. Inside, I saw Agent Jackson sitting in the usual back booth. Jackson had aged quite a bit since I'd met him back in college. I had aged too. In what seemed like the blink of an eye, we went from being young, fearless men to middle-aged with families. Maybe it was because I was walking with a cane, like an elderly man, through the diner, but I suddenly felt like I had lost so much time. Half my life spent coming to diners to report to an agent. Half my life spent living a double life.

Jackson's eyes widened when he saw me, then his expression turned dire, his face twisting into a pained mask of concern. I must've looked like a war vet, limping through the diner, grimacing in agony with every step I took. When I approached the table, he stood to greet me.

"Jesus Christ," he said. "You look like hell."

"I love you, too. You can sit, I'm fine."

We both slid into the booth. Jackson quickly waved the waiter away. We needed to be alone. As I got settled in the booth, nerve pain racked my body. Jackson sat across from me, staring, a deeply troubled look fixed on his face. I couldn't read his mind, but I felt a small part of him might feel responsible. Was it my work as an informant that nearly got me killed? Had he been reckless with my assignments? Had he put me in harm's way? It always seemed as if he'd seen me as a tool, a warm body that might someday get killed. The danger I was in always seemed like a joke to him, as if it were part of the punishment. But seeing me now, obliterated with bullet holes, he must've felt the slightest twinge of responsibility. This was the price I had paid to do his bidding.

"What happened?" he asked.

"They tried to take me out," I said. "Worst mistake they could've made was leaving me alive."

"I can't hear anything that sounds like the threat of retaliation."

"Then maybe you should close your fuckin' ears."

He dragged his hands over his face and took a deep breath. "You get a look at who it was? Any idea who's behind it?"

"Nothing solid," I said.

"A hunch?"

"It was raining, and I was wasted. Bullets flying at my head. Not sure I can trust my memory here. But one of the guys looked like this guy named Freddy who was part of Dominik's old crew."

"Dominik? Eddy's lieutenant?"

I nodded.

"He's locked up."

"He's got friends. Still wields some power in the Bluffs."

"Why would he want you dead?"

"He's always had a grudge. He blames me for the crew getting locked away. He might've heard I was an informant and figured I was the rat. Even though I wasn't. Any excuse to knock me off."

"You can't retaliate," he said. "You can't go to war."

I looked up at him but didn't say a word.

"Say something so I know you understand."

But I couldn't. Truth was, I didn't want to live in fear. As far as I knew, the guys who wanted to kill me were still out there, lurking. Plotting. Biding their time until they could finish the job. Or worse, they'd go after my family. My children. They were animals. Monsters. Madmen. They'd stop at nothing to destroy me. I wasn't going to live my life in fear. I wasn't going to spend every second of my life looking over my shoulder, checking the rearview for suspicious cars. I had every intention of getting payback. I was going to take the war to them. I needed them to know they fucked with the wrong guy.

———

Weeks vanished, lost to painkiller fog and night terrors. My life was watching TV on a couch and plotting my revenge. I had a decision to make: How far was I willing to go to get even? If it was years ago, before my kids were born, I would've gone on a belligerent tear through everyone and anyone associated with the shooters. But I had to think about my kids. There was a high likelihood one of the gunmen died in the shootout. I didn't want to end up like him or in prison. These people had stolen enough of my life. But I couldn't hide, either. I needed to let them know I wasn't going to run.

With Dominik behind bars, I knew I couldn't get to him. But he had a cousin who still lived in the Bluffs. So, on a quiet weekend morning, about six months after the shooting, I borrowed Donnie's car and took a trip into the heart of the Bluffs to pay Dominik's cousin, Anthony, a visit.

Late summer sun. Smog in the distance. Traffic backed up for miles. Sometime around six, I pulled my car to a one-story, single-family joint. Grass gone feral. Weeds overgrown. A rusted jalopy in the driveway propped on cinder blocks. Gutters falling down, dripping yesterday's rain in brown puddles on the sidewalk. I could see the TV was on through the window. I had a loaded .38 on me. This was the moment of truth: Do I bring the gun or leave it in the car? I knew how quickly this confrontation could escalate. How quickly lives get lost once guns are drawn. Far as I knew, Anthony wasn't involved in the shooting—he wasn't a gangster or one of Dominik's boys. He was just a cousin. He was somebody I could talk to and get information, a messenger I could use to deliver a threat to Dominik to back off. After a long moment of deliberation, I decided to leave my gun in the glove box.

I walked through the knee-high grass and banged loudly on the door. I knew there might be children in the house and didn't want to scare them. My desire for revenge was being balanced by my training as a cop. As an officer, my job was to deescalate. It didn't always happen. Most guys were more concerned with showing their authority. Most cops I worked with were bullies. But I had been forced to deal with many belligerent people over the years—calls of wild-eyed, drug-induced people, lost in the throes of psychosis—so I knew how to tap into that side of myself. I needed that training now. I didn't want this to escalate into a war. I just needed to find out for sure who put the hit out on me.

After the second bang, I saw him, Anthony, peeking through the window. I wouldn't expect him to recognize me. He opened the door with an agitated look on his face.

"Can you read?" he asked. "No solicitors?" He was pointing to a sign at the front of his house. I smiled. He was looking for a fight right off the bat. Typical. I took a moment to look him over. I hadn't seen the guy in a million years. Once upon a time, he'd hang out with the crew at Eddy's garage. He was Dominik's younger cousin. Never got involved as a gangster, though. He went the straight and narrow, always on the periphery of the criminal world. Chances are that his hands weren't totally clean. Guys like him were always looking to make extra scratch on the side. But he didn't have it in him to be a stone-cold killer or gangster. He was a regular joe. He had no idea what was about to happen to him.

"I'm not a Jehovah's Witness," I said. "And I ain't selling Girl Scout cookies. You don't recognize me?"

He squinted his eyes, shifted his weight, stared at me confused.

"Recognize you?"

Then a look of recognition came over his face.

"Aiden Gabor," I said. "I used to run with your cousin, Dominik, and Eddy. Back in the day."

It took him a moment to place me. Then finally, he said, "Sandwich?"

I smiled and nodded. He looked behind him, where his family was inside watching TV, probably eating dinner. "Honey, I'll be right back," he said closing the door behind him.

"Jesus, Sandwich, long time, man. The fuck you doing here?"

"I was in the neighborhood," I said. "Let's go for a walk."

He walked beside me down the driveway. "So how's your cousin?" I asked. "Heard from him lately?"

"Which one?"

"Which one? Dominik. The fat fuck."

"Oh jeez, Dom? I was just up there the other day, visiting him. He's up for parole next year."

"Is he? How nice for him. You know, I think I saw one of his buddies the other day."

"No kidding?"

"Yeah, Freddy. Remember Freddy?"

His face began to turn serious. I knew he knew something.

"I don't really keep up with those guys from the old days."

"No? You sure about that?"

"C'mon, Sandwich, what the fuck's this all about?"

A pause. A long silence. I turned, lifted my shirt to reveal the grotesque, purple scars that were rutted into my flesh from the bullets. Black stitches like a spider's web in my skin. It looked like a monster was trying to claw its way out of my body. I was a monster.

"Jesus," he said.

"Freddy and his friends paid me a visit outside Joe's Bar a couple months back. Lit me up. Tried to whack me."

"Freddy did this."

"He was one of the shooters. Any idea who gave him the order?"

As a former cop, I knew to never ask a question I didn't have the answer for. Anthony tried to play dumb.

"I don't know what you're getting at, Aiden."

I saw red. I was sick of being lied to. But I was in no shape to fight this asshole. My wounds were only half-healed. One slug to the gut and I'd go down, my body gripped in pain. But I had to send a message to Dominik. I lunged for Anthony, grabbed him by the collar, hoisted him, shifted in a semicircle, and slammed him against the car.

"The fuck you doin'?"

"I know it was your piece-of-shit cousin who ordered the hit."

"I don't know what you're talking about!"

"Tell me. Tell me who it was!"

"I don't know. I swear I don't know."

"Fuckin' liar! Tell me before I tee off on your fuckin' face."

He was crying now. Sobbing. Begging me not to hurt him. Even on offense, my body burned with nerve pain. I gritted my teeth. I couldn't let him know I was injured. I roared back and slugged him in the stomach. He keeled over and went down to a knee. I picked him back up and bitch slapped him. And again.

"You fuckin' pussy! Tell me your cousin put the hit out on me!"

He squirmed to get away. He plea-bargained with God. He wasn't cut out for this. He wasn't a gangster. He likely had never been punched in the stomach before. He begged me not to hurt him. I tightened my grip on his throat. I threatened to kill him. I threatened to bury him where nobody would find him. I didn't know if I meant it or not. It was pathetic the way he begged for help. He was guilty by association.

"Tell me the truth or they'll never find your body," I said. "Who gave the order?"

"Okay!" he finally said. "It was Dominik. He gave the order. I don't know why! I had nothing to do with it."

I only half-believed him. I chose to let him live. He curled up, fetal position, covering his face and head. I stood over him, staring down as he sobbed on the sidewalk. I knew in my heart all along it was Dominik, but having my suspicions confirmed made me hungry for revenge. I knelt down beside him with a message for his cousin. If he ever tries to come for me again, I'll kill him. If he dares to touch my family, I'll kill every person even remotely related to him. Anthony saw in my eyes that I was ready to leave dozens of bodies in my wake. I was ready to go to war.

"Tell your cousin it's over. Or I'll put him in the ground."

That was the last time I ever heard about Dominik or any of the guys from Eddy's crew.

———————

After that, things cooled down. Word on the street was Dominik heeded my warning. Or maybe he learned that it wasn't me who squealed to the feds about the crew. Whatever it was, the end result was the same: he didn't want to go to war. He tried to have me killed, and he failed.

My wounds healed with time. My bruises changed color. Eggplant to mustard to rusty brown. Barely a month after the assassination attempt, I was back at work. Back in my security uniform on the casino floor. Where had I been? I invented a cover story. "Yeah, I was down in Florida taking care of my father." I sold it. The story played. Management didn't ask questions. Nobody knew I had shrapnel in my legs and torso from the shooting. The shoot-out was a private matter. I was old-school like that. That's how Eddy taught me to be. Guys come at your guns, you bring the war home to them. You don't go running to cops or spilling your guts. It was nobody else's business.

The casino was slow. Desperation in the air. No natural light. Artificial air. Carpets from the eighties. The place needed to be renovated. A little while after I returned to work, Agent Jackson asked me to meet him at our usual spot. By that point, our communication had slowed down. The work at the casino was slow going. I figured they were moving me again. Putting me on another assignment. But it wasn't that at all. As soon as I walked into the diner, I saw him waiting at the counter. I grabbed the stool beside him. He wasted little time.

"You're free," he said.

"I'm what?"

"Free."

"Fuck's that mean?"

"It means we're cutting you loose. You're done."

I thought I was dreaming. My head was swimming. What did he mean "done"? I couldn't believe what I was hearing.

"What are you saying?"

"The department reviewed your case. It was decided that you've done your duty, and so you're cleared. You no longer have to serve as a government informant. You are a free man. Your record's been scrubbed. You're officially a civilian. Congratulations."

As the words fell from his lips, I could hardly comprehend what he was saying. This was everything I'd been waiting for since I was an eighteen-year-old freshman in college. I couldn't believe I'd been in this holding pattern for almost fifteen years. I had grown old waiting to be free again. Now that they were finally offering me my freedom, I felt a twinge of sadness. I had heard about men who spend their entire lives in prison, and once they were freed, they didn't know what to do with themselves. The only life they knew was as a prisoner. And this felt similar. I had been living two lives for so long, I didn't know any other version of myself. I was always split in two. And now, they wanted to get rid of me.

Jackson went over the logistics. The offer they made me was simple: I could go free, and they'd pay me $300,000 in a lump sum as a severance package. Or I could wait until I was fifty-five and they'd pay me four grand a month for the rest of my life. Simple as that. Cut and dry. I swallowed hard. I felt like I was taking a gulp of air for the first time in nearly twenty years. I couldn't believe how much time had passed. I could cry, or scream, or punch the wall. I had always imagined this moment. Always figured it would be the happiest of my life. But instead, I just felt confused. Where would I go? What would I do? What purpose did I serve now?

I didn't feel like I had won anything. I felt like a piece of discarded trash. I was nothing to them but a disposable hero.

———

Now that I was a free man, I only wanted one thing: family. But the money caused a rift in my family life. The money led to the third and final bombshell. It went like this:

I told Carrie that this was a settlement for me getting injured. I wanted to opt to take the smaller installments, but Carrie wanted the lump sum. After what seemed like a thousand fights, I gave in to her insistence and took the three hundred thousand. After taxes I netted just over two-thirty.

The money was supposed to last the rest of my life. It barely lasted six months. One day, not too long after they cut me loose, I was at the Cabela's looking to buy a new gun when my card was declined.

"That's impossible," I said. I rushed to the bank. I spoke to a teller. They told me I had less than a thousand dollars left in my account.

"Less than a thousand . . . how? . . . "

It had to be an error. A computer glitch. This was every dollar I had in the world, suddenly gone. Vanished overnight. And that's when they dropped the hammer: my wife, Carrie, had taken the money out. I floored my car home and went barging into the house. Carrie was cowering in the corner.

"What the fuck did you do?"

I punched three holes in the kitchen wall. She fought me back. She had given the money to her sister. She wouldn't tell me why. I threatened to kill her. She threatened to call the police. She locked me out of our bedroom. She packed her bags and called a cab. I paced the living room. It was an unforgiveable betrayal, and I knew our marriage would never survive it. When she left that afternoon, I knew my marriage was over.

After Carrie left, I learned about her secret infidelities. She'd been cheating on me for the last couple years while I was far away at work. She had been giving money away to her sister and family throughout our time together that I was not aware of.

I went off the deep end. Drinking myself into night stupors. Everything seemed to be falling apart. My idol was dead and in the ground. I'd lost my marriage and my purpose; I had no idea who I was anymore. I was thrown to the side like garbage by the DOJ after they got what they wanted. I was drifting aimlessly through life, unsure of what would become of me. I wasn't even sure if I wanted to live anymore.

Things would get worse before they got better. A few months after Carrie and I split for good, I received a call from Donnie. I was half in the bag. I was about to call it a night.

"What're you calling me this late for?" I asked.

"We got your kid down here in cuffs."

I knew I misheard him.

"My kid?"

"Your son," he said. "Chris."

That's impossible, I thought. My son was twelve years old. He was a good kid. He wouldn't hurt a fly.

"Fuck off," I said. "What do you mean you got Chris down there in cuffs? What for?"

"They nabbed him for stealing a car," he said.

It couldn't be true. I stood up frantic. Family was all I wanted. And now my family was under fire.

CHAPTER 12

A hush came over the station house. Radios chirped out static crackle codes. I stared at my son through the bulletproof glass.

He was hunched on the bench. Face hidden by his hoody.

All around me, radios were chirping out burglaries and domestic disputes. Plainclothes cops carried Styrofoam coffee cups, with stacks of paperwork tucked under their arms. Drunk tank regulars were crowded in the holding cells. The cinder-block station house was suffocating. Truth be told, I missed it. The rush of a new call. The surge of adrenaline that came with responding to an emergency. Every night your life is on the line. But it wasn't anywhere for a twelve-year-old boy. As I stood there, motionless, half in shock, looking at my youngest son through the glass, I couldn't believe what was happening. I had finally broken free from the system that destroyed my life. The endless cycle of crime and incarceration that came to define me. Only to watch my son get swept up into it. It couldn't be happening. The kid was in seventh grade. I could not allow him to go down the same path that I did.

The metal door scraped the concrete floor as I pushed my way into the small interrogation room. My kid sat in a chair behind a long metal desk. Arms folded. Eyes fixed to the floor. I couldn't tell if his pouting demeanor was born out of guilt or shame. Or maybe it was defiance. If this kid had inherited my stubbornness and criminality, I had only myself to blame. It was like I had stepped through a time warp and was facing off with my younger self. What would I tell twelve-year-old me if I had a chance to step back in time and intervene?

I shut the door hard behind me. Rolled up my sleeves. I'd done this a time or two—grilled a perp, strong-armed some criminal. Back in my day on the force, I'd been known to slap a guy around to get a confession. But never in my worst nightmares did I ever think I'd be alone inside that room with my own son.

Christopher looked up at me. His eyes were half-covered in the shadows from his hood. His eyes were a mixture of sorry and blank or scared and uncaring. His eyes harbored secrets. They were harder to read than mine were. He had a frightened look on his face. His bottom lip quivered as I pulled out the chair to take a seat. From this distance, I could feel the nervous energy radiating from his body. He looked like a child. And then something dawned on me: he was the same age I was when I started working for Eddy. I was a child when I started running packages for the Mafia. I didn't feel like a kid at the time. I felt like a little man. But I was a child. It wasn't until that moment that I was able to fully appreciate just how young and scared and lost and desperate I had been for family. For a father. To feel like I was a part of something.

But that was my story—my legacy. I couldn't let it become the legacy of my son. He didn't know about my past stealing cars. I had done my best to shield him from the life I used to lead. And yet still it permeated our lives. It was almost as if being a criminal was hereditary. I got it from my father, and now Chris had gotten it from me. I wouldn't stand for it. The cycle needed to end.

"I'm sorry, Dad," Chris said, in a meek, trembling voice.

"Shut up. You're lucky I don't break your fuckin' face for what you did. What the fuck were you thinking? Stealing a car? You think you're some kinda tough guy?"

"I didn't do shit!"

"Oh, you're gonna talk back? You wanna spend the rest of your life in juvie? Is that it?"

"No."

"Listen to me. I'm not gonna sit back and watch as you throw your life away, you hear me? You're gonna go to court, and you're gonna face whatever consequences the judge decides. Understand? And you better thank God you're under eighteen because if you weren't this would be on your permanent record."

"But . . . "

"Don't say a goddamn word. Just nod and say you understand."

Chris looked up at me defiantly. I could see his nostrils flare. The intensity in his eyes was the same I had at his age. At times, looking at the kid was like looking at a photograph of myself when I was twelve.

"I understand," he finally said. "Are you gonna tell Mom?"

"Yes. And I'm gonna take you home and you're gonna explain what happened. The only way you'll learn is if you face the consequences of what you've done."

In the end, the kid wasn't too different from me. He was young and naïve and lured into the mob by promises of easy money. But he had something I never did—he had a father who had already made those mistakes. By seeing me, he saw all the ways working with the Mafia can wreck your life.

Months and months later, when the court date finally arrived, the judge let Chris off with just a warning. I was livid at his leniency. His reasoning was that the kids were found by the police sitting in the car while the car was parked and the engine was off. Had the cops caught them driving and pulled them over, the consequences would be more severe. As it stood, the cops didn't have much to go on. My kid had lucked into a legal loophole. He got lucky. He also didn't learn. I wanted him to feel the sting of justice. I needed him to know how quickly the jaws of justice can clamp down around you. I was scared that by letting him off the courts were giving him permission to do it again. Crime is a drug. That first high is such a rush. You spend the rest of your life chasing that feeling, that surge. I didn't want it to consume him the way it consumed me.

We left the courthouse that day in tense silence. He was only in seventh grade— how was this happening already? Inside the car, he turned the radio on. I clicked it right off.

"Listen to me," I said. "Look me in the eye and swear you're done with all this bullshit."

"Dad, c'mon . . . "

"Chris, look at me. I wanna hear you say you're finished. You got lucky today. Next time you won't. Promise me there'll be no next time."

He paused a moment. "I promise, Dad."

It was a promise he couldn't keep. Deep inside I knew what was coming. This was only the beginning of my son's descent into crime.

I kept working. I needed money. Needed a purpose, some reason to keep going. And the paycheck I was getting from the casino was steady. I knew I'd never get rich doing it, but I kept plugging away. About a year after the shooting, I got a call from one of my managers that a mysterious fire swept through the casino. I sat up in bed.

"A fire?"

"We might lose the whole place!" he said. Turns out, a fire started in the basement and wiped out all the records, charring the walls and decimating a majority of the building. The actual casino floor wasn't too badly damaged, but they were closing their doors for four to six months. Given the corrupt nature of casinos and their mob ties, the fire caught the eyes of arson investigators. With the casino being closed for the foreseeable future, upper management rented out the conference space of a nearby hotel and decided to hold a series of trainings: safety, sensitivity, and sexual harassment. The way I saw it, if they wanted to pay me to sit in the dark and sleep through some lame instructional film on how not to offend my coworkers, be my guest.

Monday. Eight a.m. sharp. The trainings began bright and early. By noon, I'd hit a wall. The after-lunch lull. Boardroom boredom. Midday blues. I was twiddling my thumbs, tapping a cup of tepid coffee on the tabletop, ready for a nap, counting the seconds until I could go home, waiting for the next mandatory sensitivity training to begin.

And then . . . boom! That's when everything changed, again. A shining white light went blaring on inside of my mind. The boardroom door opened and in walked the most beautiful woman I'd ever seen in my life. It was as if the entire world went dark around me, blurred and out of focus, and the only thing I could see was her. She was stunning—and I stared at her with my mouth open, as if I were a bird-watcher who'd just seen the rarest species of condor. Was it just my imagination of was she floating on air? It seemed that way. Seeing her there was similar to taking a gunshot to the chest. I was short of breath, light-headed. Most of all I was nervous. I felt as if I was being plunged into a feeling I'd never had before. Call it love at first sight. Call it what you want. All I know is I couldn't take my eyes off her.

Certain as I was that I'd never seen her before, I was also overwhelmed with this unshakable feeling that I had known her my entire life. How could I be in love with somebody I'd never spoken to? How could I be so sure of my feelings of a person I'd only just seen from a distance? I had been married for over a decade and never once felt this cannonball rush of stupid, giddy love.

I swallowed hard. I knew what I had to do. I had to find some clever reason to talk to her. I had to know everything about her. What was her name? What did she do? I had doubted since I was a teenager that God had any sort of plan for me on this Earth, but sitting there in that boardroom, it seemed like every mistake, every fight, every gamble I ever made and survived, had led me to this moment. I was supposed to be sitting there in that boardroom because I was meant to meet this woman.

I leaned to my right and nudged my buddy in the ribs, then gestured at the front of the room with my head.

"Who is that?" I asked my buddy.

"Who? Sabrina?" my buddy whispered. "Don't even think about it. She's a bitch."

I stared at him with a homicidal look in my eyes. I didn't even know this woman and I was ready to kill for her. I felt the urge to slam his face into the desk and break his face against the varnished wood finish. But I didn't care what he said. I barely even heard him. I was too dumbstruck. I was giddy. What were the odds this beautiful woman worked at this casino where I had? How had I never seen her before this moment? I couldn't take my eyes off her.

She was in finance.

The lecture ran over. She stopped the projector and flicked on the lights. I squinted at the blinding fluorescence. After everyone started shuffling out, I got up the courage to approach her.

"Nice speech," I said. "I'm Aiden."

"Sabrina," she said.

"Forgive me for being so forward," I said, "but you have the most beautiful eyes in the world." Except I wasn't staring at her eyes. I was staring directly at her breasts. This kind of sophomoric joke is the kind of thing I'd pulled with another woman. A litmus test of sorts to see how much of my bullshit they'd be willing to take. Turns out, she had a low threshold for immature bullshit. I looked back up at her to see a stone-cold, unamused death stare. God, she looked so familiar to me. Why couldn't I place her face?

"My eyes are up here," she said.

"C'mon, where's your sense of humor?"

"I guess I'm not like the other girls you've tried to hit on."

She feigned disinterest with a hard-to-get smirk. She seemed impervious to my alleged charm. Stonewalled my jokes. She was tougher than the women I had typically hit on. This only confirmed what I already knew: she was the one.

I followed her to the coffee machine. Readjusted my dress shirt and my approach.

"Look, can we start over? I'm not an asshole, I promise. That was just a stupid joke I used to pull with my buddies."

She mulled it over a moment. "What do you do for the casino?" she asked.

"Security."

"Ironic," she said. "Your jokes make you seem insecure."

I smiled. She was a killer. She was the type of woman who could go toe-to-toe with a guy like me. Someone who could take it and give it right back. I wanted to know what made her skin so thick. I wanted to know everything about her.

"Okay, I deserved that," I said. "Since I already messed up, why don't you let me take you to dinner."

"Why would I do that?"

"We both have to eat. What do you say?"

"Can I think about it?"

It took almost five months of me trying, but she finally agreed to dinner.

———————

Date night. Seven p.m. I was running late. I threw on the only clean shirt I could find. Half wrinkled. Folded up my cuffs. Pushed my hair back with my hands. It didn't occur to me until that moment, but I hadn't been on a first date like this in nearly twenty years. I had been so many people between then and now I wasn't sure who I was anymore. I didn't know if I still had it or not.

She lived near the casino. I drove out from the Bluffs to pick her up at half past eight. She was waiting outside in the cold. She was shivering in place. She wore a blue, knee-length dress, a light windbreaker, and a pair of glasses that floored me. She was smart and sexy in a way I'd never seen before. Curves in all the right places. I stole glances at her in the car. The light from the moon lit her face.

Over to Main Street. A bar not far from her place. A cramped, low-lit dive known for its burgers. Sabrina ordered a beer. I nursed a tap water, no ice. She asked me if I was sober. I said I stopped drinking a couple years ago, but I didn't go into detail. It was the shooting that ultimately led to my sobriety, but I was hesitant to overshare on a first date. My expression said, "Don't ask." Don't tug at loose threads on the first date. I didn't like being in the hot seat. I was a former cop; I preferred to be in charge. I wanted to ask the questions.

Dinner lasted three hours. We couldn't stop talking. We couldn't have been more different. She was a brainy, quiet little thing, at least that's what I thought. She would prove me wrong on that one. I was a brutish, loud barbarian of a man. But there was something undeniable between us. Over shared appetizers, I learned she studied at the University of Wisconsin. She had a master's in marketing. Worked in child services. Worked for Kellogg's. She seemed to have lived ten different lives. Anytime she tried to turn the topic to me, I resisted. I deflected. I did whatever I could to pull focus.

"You don't like talking about yourself?" she finally asked.

I didn't. My life was a collection of secrets. I always had something to hide. I couldn't tell her about my past in the Mafia. I couldn't tell her I'd been an informant for a decade. I didn't want her to know about the gunfights I'd survived or the sadistic crimes I'd been a part of. Nothing in my life was conversation fodder for a first date. I was more comfortable sharing the facade.

"I guess we'll have to take it slow," I said.

Just then, I saw Sabrina notice someone near the front of the bar. A tall, skinny guy came striding over to our table. She introduced him as her ex-fiancé. He shook my hand. Shook hers. We made small talk for a bit. Then, I noticed a tear coming from her eye, which was very out of character for her. If nothing else, Sabrina was tough. This man must have really done something to hurt her. Inside I started to boil. I felt myself reverting into the old me. I thought I had outgrown this violent streak. I thought the shooting slowed me down. Calmed me down. In the old days, I would've taken the guy outside and beaten the shit out of him for no reason. Just being her ex was enough to light the fuse. The old me would've perceived this seemingly innocent run-in as an intentional act of disrespect. I'd be so enraged that I'd need to drag this asshole outside by the hair and smash his face in just to show her that I was the kind of man you don't try to humiliate.

I flashed back to the night I met Carrie—years before we were married—and how turned on and impressed she had been when I beat the shit out of a total stranger who slighted me. My only experience with women—with alleged love—was that it was born out of violence. I attracted women who were attracted to violent men. I thought it was how I got women to like me.

I stood up and excused myself. I acted like I was going to the bathroom. He was standing by the front door. Soon as I got close enough to him, I bum-rushed him and shoved him outside and slammed him up against the hood of a parked car. I grabbed him by the shirt collar and slammed him two, three times into the door.

"Get your fuckin' hands off me," he yelled. But I was seeing red. I wanted Sabrina to see this side of me. I wanted her to know what a pussy her ex was compared to me. I was going to beat his skull in right there.

I slugged him once in the gut and he crumpled to a knee.

"Aiden, what the fuck are you doing!" she yelled.

"Stay out of this!"

But she didn't stay out of it. Instead, she did something I had never seen a woman do. She stepped between us. She had a fierceness in her eyes I hadn't seen since my own mother. She demanded I stop. For any other woman, I would've said no. But I saw something in Sabrina's eyes. I felt something. I felt like a pit bull being reined in by its owner.

"Knock it the fuck off!" she yelled.

She backed me up. Her ex looked up at me with hurt, confused eyes.

"Let him go. Stop your bullshit. Now!"

I don't know what it was about her, but she had this power over me. And to my own shock, I did what she said. I stepped back. I let off him. I didn't make another move.

Sabrina paid the bill. Apologized to the manager. Her ex didn't want the cops involved. She rushed off in a huff to the car. I followed. I didn't start the engine. Instead, we sat in the tension. I did it again. I sabotaged another relationship. It's what I'd been doing my entire life. Now that she had gotten a glimpse into the real me—violent, impulsive—I knew she would leave. She would hightail it out. She would do what she should do and run. I didn't know it in the moment, but it was my way of proving to myself that I didn't deserve to be loved in a healthy way. The only love I had ever known was toxic, anxious, jealous love. You couldn't even call it love. With Carrie, I was constantly trying to prove my masculinity. It wasn't a marriage; it was a power struggle. But Sabrina was different. She didn't have any patience for this side of me. In the past, my violent side had impressed the women I dated. It only seemed to repulse Sabrina.

After taking a moment to regain her composure, Sabrina cleared her throat and tried to speak.

"What the hell was that all about?" she asked.

I stayed on the defensive.

"Little miss prim," I said, shaking my head. "You're making too big a deal about it. So I roughed him up a little."

"No," she said. "You embarrassed me. And you embarrassed yourself. If you're going to be with me, you won't be going around hitting every guy who looks at me."

I diverted my eyes. Shame forced them downward.

"Look me in the eye," she said. Hearing her say that brought me back to the conversation I had at the police house with my son Chris. He couldn't look me in the eye. And just as I touched his chin to position his face to look at me, she did the same to me. She lifted my head until my eyes were level with hers.

"I don't know what it is, but I know there's more to you than you're telling me. I can see it in your eyes. But if there's gonna be a second date, and a third, you're going to have to open up. And you're gonna promise me you'll never do what you did tonight ever again."

My gut said to bail. My heart said to fight for her. My heart knew it didn't want to lose this girl. I barely knew her, but she saw something in me even I didn't know was there. She didn't see the man I was—she saw the man I could be. I worried she was in over her head. She was trying to domesticate a wild animal. I was a rabid dog, and she was trying to make me heel and obey. But my love for her was greater than my stubborn pride. I wanted to be the man she knew I could be. So I nodded. I promised her I would try to do better.

I would do it for her. I would do it for me.

CHAPTER 13

P eople don't change overnight. I was no exception. I was committed to being a better man. I tried to put the past behind me. Sabrina and I took it slow. We dated. We spoke for hours on the phone. I felt like a monster, frozen in a block of ice, and Sabrina had an ice pick, whittling away at my icy exterior, trying to find the man underneath. I wasn't so sure he was alive inside of the ice block. She seemed certain he was.

People always said boys marry someone like their mom. Carrie certainly was nothing like my mom. Sabrina, on the other hand, was exactly like my mother. She loved to cook, loved to go out on adventures, and loved being around people. She was sassy and took shit from no one, the first one to stand up and defend another.

A few months after our first date, it was time to meet the family. It started with her father, then her beloved Uncle Michael. Uncle Mike drove east from the Midwest. Stayed a few nights on the pullout. I wasn't too fond of family visits. I never got along well with Carrie's family. I was nervous to meet Sabrina's tribe. Uncle Mike was a good enough guy. A retired police officer. Soft-spoken and cordial. Sabrina loved him like a father. If she loved him, then I loved him. His first night in town, we had dinner. Shared war stories. Inevitably, my former life as a cop came up. Toward the end of the meal, while Sabrina was busy doing the dishes, Mike got a quizzical look on his face.

"Gabor," he kept saying. "That's a pretty unusual name. Where have I heard it before?"

I shrugged. Beats me.

"Were you ever a cop in Blue Bell?"

I stopped and turned with a curious look fixed on my face.

"Yeah . . . "

How could he know all these details? Something wasn't right. It was my instinct to think he was up to no good. Did he know the guys I ran with in the Bluffs? What was he angling at?

"Yeah, I worked in Blue Bell for about a year. My first year as a cop."

"Holy shit," he said. "It was you."

I squinted, half confused. More than a little worried. "What was me?"

"You were the cop that arrested Sabrina when she was fifteen years old."

"I think you might've had a little too much to drink," I said.

"No, no. I'm dead serious. Did you ever bust a teenage girl at a bar?"

"Every night of my career," I said. "You think I'm gonna remember twenty years ago?"

"C'mon, think," he said. Then he called Sabrina into the room. "Pumpkin, what was the name of the bar you got arrested at? In Blue Bell. You remember?"

Sabrina came in, drying her hands on a dish towel. She was searching her memory. Then finally she came out with it: the Brickyard.

It floored me. No way in hell. All of a sudden, a memory came flooding back.

I was a young beat cop. Just starting out. First few weeks on the force in Blue Bell. The dispatcher's voice came crackling through. A crisis at a college bar. I was riding solo. Single-man unit. Didn't need my siren for this. Seemed like a routine, minor call.

The bar was called the Brickyard. The bar had a slight reputation: it was a pickup joint where kids from a few different colleges came together to drink and smoke pot. Inside it was rowdy for a weekday. The stench of spilled beer. College kids playing darts. Van Halen on the jukebox. I leaned on the bar and yelled over the music.

"I'm looking for the manager."

"Lou," the kid said and pointed me to the back.

As I made my way through the obstacle course of tables and barstools, the patrons were eyeing me. Anytime I went anywhere in uniform, I got stares. Cops always do. The presence of a cop looms large. To see a cop is to know there's danger nearby.

Toward the back of the bar, by the kitchen area, I saw a man in plain clothes who looked like a manager. He was irate.

"Christ, I called ten minutes ago. Fuck took you so long?"

"What's the problem?" I asked.

"This one here," he said. He pointed at a young girl, sitting in a chair. Hands folded in her lap. Head bowed with soft, auburn hair in her face. She seemed to me like she couldn't hurt a fly. What could she have possibly done? "She comes in here with a fake ID. We bust them here. She's lying about her name. Then she attacks my security guard."

She looked up at me through the hair that had fallen in front of her face. Then I looked at the security guard: guy was six-foot-six. Two-twenty. Tatted-up retired cop who worked security to make extra scratch on the weekends. It looked like he could wrestle a bear and he was crying because some girl attacked him.

"She attacked him?" I asked. "He's three times her size."

"She shouldn't be in here. I want her arrested for trespassing, resisting arrest, and assaulting an officer."

"Resisting?" I said. "You gotta be kidding me, she's a damn kid."

It wasn't clear why the manager had such animosity toward this girl. All I knew was, I had to get her out of there to somewhere a bit safer.

I walked over to the girl and knelt down. At this distance, she looked twenty, but something about her told me she was younger than that. Maybe it was the look in her eyes that made her seem like a child. Even though she looked older, I pegged her at fifteen or sixteen. A high schooler trying to pass as an adult. A kid with no business in a pickup bar.

I was just twenty-one myself and knew my way around a fake ID. I had a bit of sympathy for the kid.

"You sneak in here with a fake ID?" I asked.

She gave me a dirty look but didn't answer.

"So, it's gonna be like that, huh?"

She shrugged. She was tough. This was going to be more difficult than I thought.

"All right, why don't you and me go for a ride to the precinct?"

———————

I told her to watch her head as I put her in the police car. She rode in the back while I drove. It was only a ten-minute drive to the precinct, but I decided to take the long way. I wanted to see if I could get her to talk.

"Awfully young for hitting up a bar," I said.

"I'm twenty-one," she said. "Going on twenty-two."

She was lying again.

"You go to school?" I asked her.

"Maybe."

She played her cards close to her chest. She was a real treat.

"You know, if you go to college and get busted for underage drinking, they'll take your scholarship from you."

A pause.

"You don't gotta worry about me," she said.

I smiled and shook my head, half bemused, half irritated. There was a fine line between playful teasing and evading the questions of a police officer. I wanted to give her the benefit of the doubt. She was young. On her own. And even if she didn't show it, she was likely scared half to death. As I pulled into the precinct parking lot, I glanced back at her in the rearview mirror.

"What did you say your name was?"

She was quiet, hesitant to answer. I parked and killed the engine. Looked back at her. She was staring back at me defiantly.

"Not gonna tell me, huh? All right, let's get you fingerprinted."

The police house hummed with calm and boredom. The everydayness of mundane, small-town police work. The peck of keyboards. The buzzing of a vending machine. Stale, recycled air. A football game on TV. I led this mystery girl through the lobby and into the precinct and into the back.

"Gabor, who's the collar?" my chief yelled out.

"Underage kid," I said. "Got her sneaking into a bar. No ID. Gonna seventy-two her until I figure out who she is."

The police lingo must've spooked her. Her eyes darted up at me.

"Seventy-two?" she asked. "What's that?"

"It's when they keep you in a holding cell for three days while we figure out your name and where you live. Then we call somebody to come get you. I'm gonna take your picture," I said. "For our records."

"Okay, you do what you think you need to do," she said with a devilish look. "When do I get my phone call, please?"

Her cavalier attitude was really pissing me off. I didn't want to deal with this one anymore and handed her off to get photographed.

I went back an hour later and I could not find her.

"Hey, chief, where is that underage that I just brought in?"

Chief responded, "She was a friend of our family, you know how that goes."

The realization that I had arrested Sabrina nearly twenty years before I took her on a first date only confirmed what I already knew: she was my soulmate. We were destined to meet. And she was just as sassy now.

———

I blinked and five years passed. Carrie finally granted me the divorce I'd been seeking. Sabrina and I fell deeper and deeper in love. Meanwhile, Chris fell deeper into crime. At seventeen, he was stealing cars just like his old man. By this point I had left the casino for good and started picking up some shifts as a manager at an Applebee's. Anything to keep me busy and bring in a little extra dough. I was a civilian in the suburbs. I had finally made it out of the Bluffs. But the Bluffs were like quicksand, and now they had a grip on my son, dragging him under, sucking him into the endless abyss of crime.

My son Chris was seventeen. He was living with his mom and his brother in the Bluffs. Up to that point, the kid had managed to escape jail. The cops hadn't caught up with him. Not yet. Now and then, I'd hear snippets of gossip through the Mafia grapevine. Or cop friends would get wind of some carjacking they suspected Chris to be involved in. I felt like he was slipping away from me. I hated seeing him repeating the sins of my past. I thought I had done everything to keep my kid's nose clean, but he just couldn't stay away. A part of me wanted to stay out of it. Maybe he needed to hit rock bottom. Just like you'd do with an addict, I couldn't enable him. I had to let him live his life. But then, my past finally caught up with me.

Donnie Cooper called me up.

"You hear about Chris?" he asked.

"What now?"

"Saw him hanging out with Joey Sasso."

Joey Sasso? My heart sank in my chest. I stood, fists shaking, nostrils flaring. I was so angry I thought blood might start pouring out my ears. Joey Sasso was an old friend from the Bluffs. An old mob buddy from Eddy's crew. He was a made guy. He ran low-rent scams around town. Dabbled in carjackings. A classic crook. But the gall of that man to try and recruit my son! My son! Did that piece of shit really think he could enlist my son to do his dirty work? Was he out of his fucking mind? I was lit. I was livid. If the mobsters from the Bluffs wanted to whack me, so be it. I didn't care about my own life. But I'd be damned if they were gonna corrupt my youngest son.

Carrie got the kids. I saw them on weekends and every other Wednesday. I'd pick them up from school. Most of our visits, we'd go to movies or I'd let them run around an arcade for a few hours.

One night, just before I dropped them off, I sent Nolan in ahead and asked Chris to wait back. I needed to talk to him.

"What's this all about?" he asked.

"Some friends of mine saw you with Uncle Joey."

"So?"

"So? Were you gonna tell me you saw him?"

"Is it any of your business?"

I smirked at the balls on this kid. He was on my last nerve.

"What were you doing with him?" I asked.

"Making a little extra cash," he said. "Like you used to do."

"You don't know anything about what I used to do," I said. "What kinda work are you doing for him?"

"Jesus, Dad, nothing. Just running some packages."

"What's in the packages, Chris?"

"I don't know. He just gives them to me and I deliver them."

"Are you fucking stupid?"

"What?"

"There could be fuckin' dope in those packages. Bricks of heroin. Or illegal guns. You got no idea what you're delivering. You know what happens if you get caught schlepping drugs or guns across the city? We're talking serious prison time. We're talking the end of your life. You wanna throw everything away the same way I did? You think this is a joke?"

"God, you're so dramatic," he said. "It's not that big of a deal."

I took a deep breath. I was shaking, either from sadness or fury, I couldn't tell which. I reached into the passenger seat and grabbed my son by the wrist. I could feel his heartbeat in my palm. It brought me back to the days when he was still a baby and I'd listen to his heart beat so softly in his chest. He was so pure back then. So innocent.

"Listen to me," I said. "This life. This criminal life. It might seem like easy money. It might seem like these guys care about you. But they don't, Chris. They say they're

a family, but when push comes to shove, they'll sell you out and only protect themselves. You aren't their blood. Look at me."

I touched his chin with my fingers to get him to raise his eyes.

"Look me in the eye. I'm your blood. Like it or not, I'm what you're stuck with. And
I'm begging you not to do this."

Chris stared blankly at me. It was a look I recognized all too well. It was that pigheadedness he'd inherited from me.

"So it's okay for you to run around with Uncle Eddy, doing whatever you want,
making money, but it's not okay for me?"

"It wasn't okay for me," I said. "I was a stupid, lonely kid who thought this shit was
my only way to having the life I wanted. I wasn't ever any good at school. I didn't know
better. But you? You could do anything you set your mind to. You're better than me,
kiddo. I made those mistakes already. And I vowed I'd never let you make the same
ones I did. So I'm begging you, don't do this. Don't throw your life away."

I no longer knew if I was talking to Chris or talking to my younger self. A part of
me imagined nineteen-year-old Aiden Gabor, sitting on the couch, listening to every
word I said. What I wouldn't do to go back in time and slap him around and talk some
sense into him. But there was another layer to our interaction. As I knelt beside my
son, I realized that I went through everything I did—survived it all—for this moment.
I needed to learn those lessons so I could prevent my son from going down that dark
road of crime.

"Okay," he said.

"Okay, what?"

"I'll stop," he said. "If you don't want me running with Uncle Joey, I won't. I'll give
it up."

I wasn't finished so quick. That night, I drove my motorcycle to the backstreets of the
Bluffs. It was time to put this city in my rearview for good. I pulled up to Joey's house.
Killed the engine, killed the headlights. Tilted the bike on its kickstand and walked
with purpose to the front door. It was ten at night, but what did I care? I loitered out
front. I let my rage consume me. I banged hard on the door with a cold, closed fist.

The porch light got tripped. Joey's beady eyes poked through the curtains.

"Who is it?"

"It's Aiden," I said. "Open the door?"

"Sandwich?"

Only guys from Eddy's crew called me Sandwich. Whenever I'd hear the name, it would bring me right back to my days as a mobster. How long ago all that felt now. Standing there, it was hard to believe I had a kid old enough to be jacking cars and running packages. Where did the time go?

Joey opened the door. He was a slob in a dirty white undershirt. His hair was disheveled. He hadn't shaved in days.

"Been a long time," he said. "You don't call. Just show up outta the blue. Ain't it a little late for a drop-in? Fuck you doing here?"

"We need to talk."

"Now?"

He cocked his head, unsure. I couldn't tell if he was playing dumb. Historically, the guy was a dumb fuck, so it wasn't always easy to tell.

"You got my kid running packages?" I asked.

"Is that what this is about?" he asked. "Why don't you come inside, we'll talk."

I followed him in. He closed the door.

"Answer the question," I said.

Joey smiled and shrugged.

"Aiden, c'mon. How long we known each other? The kid came to me looking to make a little extra scratch. That's all. I thought I was doing you a favor."

"A favor?"

I grabbed him by the throat and slammed him up against the stairway banister. To grab a made guy like that was tantamount to a death sentence. It was something you just didn't do. But he was meddling with my family, and family was all I had left. I needed to send him a message.

"Listen to me," I said. "You leave my son alone. I find out you're courting him for jobs, and I swear to God, Joey, I'll bury you. I'll bury you in the middle of nowhere where nobody'll ever find you. You even breathe in his direction again, and I'll fuckin' kill you."

"You fuckin' crazy?" he yelled. "Puttin' your hands on a made guy. You know who the fuck I am?"

"I do. I know exactly who you are. And you know who I am. Next time, you won't even see me coming. You leave my son alone."

And that was that. I left him there on the ground. Walked to my bike. Revved the engine and screeched my way down the block. That was the last time I ever rode through the Bluffs. Block by block, the city faded in my rearview mirror. I cranked the gas harder, riding like death was chasing me, finally escaping the Bluffs. Finally leaving the city in the past.

CHAPTER 14

That should've been how my story ended. Standing tall, high on a hill, watching the Bluffs disappear behind me. God had other plans.

After the confrontation with Joey, life quieted down. I wasn't a gangster. I wasn't a cop. So what was I? My kids were living with their mom. Chris stopped stealing cars and finally went back to school. I moved into a charming, one-story house with Sabrina. This was civilian life. This was settling down in the suburbs. For the first time, life began to seem normal. It was the kind of boring I welcomed. After a life of living with panic in my chest, I reveled in the silence of our small suburban town. It felt a bit like witness protection. It was a slower pace than I was used to but I was happy. One night, after a late shift at Applebee's, I stopped off at Walmart on the way home to pick up some chips and diet soda. Even at midnight, the fluorescent lights were beating down like sunrays. Somewhere down that wide aisle, I started feeling this dull, low-grade pain in my chest. I ignored it.

I kept shopping.

Threw a few more items into my cart and felt that throbbing again. It wasn't a pain I was familiar with. I began to push my cart to the front of the store. Hit the self-checkout.

Something was wrong.

I drove twelve blocks with a pain shooting through my arm. Back at home, I set the groceries on the counter.

"How was work?" Sabrina asked, eyes glued to the TV set.

"Fine," I said. "Same. I'm turning in early. Not feeling so great."

But as I lay in bed, the pain in my chest only swelled. A shooting pain went spiking through my left arm. I felt paralyzed. My body was locking up. Jammed up. I couldn't move. Shortness of breath. Vision was blurring. Couldn't get any air into my lungs. Couldn't get oxygen to my brain.

With every ounce of energy I had left, I called for Sabrina.

"Sabrina, get me something for pain, could you?"

"What's wrong?" she questioned, coming into the room.

"My arm is hurting and now my jaw is starting to hurt, like I just got into a fight."

"Jesus Christ," she said. "We gotta get you to the hospital. I think you are having a fucking heart attack."

Less than ten minutes later, she went screeching into the emergency parking lot with me clutching my arm in the passenger seat. She dragged me inside, screaming for the nurses to help.

"I think he's having a heart attack," she yelled.

The ER nurses rushed me into a white room and ran an EKG. I gulped for breath. I wasn't going to make it. The machine spit out a piece of monitoring paper scribbled with zigzagging lines. The doctor snagged the paper and read it. Then she blanched white as a blankness came over her face.

"Mr. Gabor," she said. "You're having a heart attack."

That's when everything went black.

CHAPTER 15

Nurses, sirens, IV drips. I opened my eyes to the fog of purgatory. Lab coats hovered over me. Were they doctors or angels? In my half-conscious state, I couldn't tell. I was doped up on liquid drugs. Meds and morphine clouded my brain. My vision ebbed in and out of focus. I was drenched in white: white light, white coats, white paper gowns. Tubes snaking into my arms, feeding me morphine. I could only recall broken fragments of memory: ER nurses pushing me on a gurney down a hallway tracked with mud. The blur of cylinder ceiling lights. I remembered crashing through the double doors of the ICU. Hallways clogged with gurneys. White coats all around. I was gasping on a stretcher. Staring at the ceiling lights. Sabrina was there with me. They asked me to count backward from ten. All I knew, I died on the spot. The world went black. Then white. Just when I had finally found happiness, God went and struck me down. It was almost as if he were waiting for me to be happy. Waiting like a snake coiled in the grass, biding His time for the patient moment to act. White always means death.

And then I woke up to two dozen strangers holding clipboards, staring at me like I was an animal at the zoo.

Yes, I decided. This must be hell.

"Morning, Aiden. I'm Dr. Lopez. Head cardiologist. How are you feeling?"

Everything was white and blurry. I tried to sit up and my paper gown crinkled.

"Where am I?" I asked.

"You're at the Rutgers University Hospital," he said. "You've just successfully completed an angioplasty. These people around you are interns in the cardiology department."

"Are you shittin' me?"

"No, I'm certainly not," he said. "Why don't you take a look up here."

The screen looked something like an ultrasound. Like a moving X-ray of liquid metal.

"This is your heart," he said. "Congratulations, you survived a widow-maker."

"A what?"

"You had a heart attack. Only three percent of people survive what you had. Are you feeling lucky?"

"Maybe I should go to Vegas," I said.

"I think you may have used up all your luck on this one," he said.

Then he said something that didn't mean much to me at the time. "God must have kept you here for a reason." I had never been a religious guy. I made fun of Sammy, my childhood friend, for being Jewish, and you wouldn't catch me dead in a church except for a wedding or a funeral. Even at that moment, after being granted an extra chance at life, I still wasn't ready to change. Looking back, though, I know he was right. God did save my life for a reason.

───────────

The room I was stuck in was enormous—large enough to fit twenty hospital beds. I was the only person there. Light poured in from the windows. White curtains billowed like ghosts. I still couldn't understand why there were so many people in the room. Dr. Lopez pointed to the TV screen with a pen. He explained to me that they performed an angioplasty. They put a tube in my leg and fished it through my abdomen to my heart. They then put two stents in my heart.

"There was a lot of damage to the bottom of your heart," he said, motioning to the screen with his pen. "The bottom of the heart contains about fifty percent of the muscle. You're lucky you got here in time."

"My girlfriend insisted I come," I said.

"Then you need to tell your girlfriend she saved your life."

As I slowly got my bearings, I gestured for the doctor to come closer.

"Where's Sabrina?" I asked.

"She's been in the waiting room all night. She never went home. She never left your side while you were out."

I smirked with a shrug. Even though I'd been unconscious I knew she was there. I could feel her. I had only been this close to death one other time: after the shooting. Back then, I was too scared to go to the hospital. I recovered by myself in the basement of a friend, too scared to tell my then-wife. But now, I had Sabrina. I had a woman who loved me in my corner. And even if that heart attack had taken me, I would not have been alone. I'd never be alone again.

I waved the doctor in again. "One more thing, doc. Who the fuck are all these people?"

"Oh, this is a teaching hospital," he said. "These are all med students. Your heart attack is helping train an entire class of hopeful doctors."

I stayed in the hospital for seven days. They moved me to a private room. A couple days after my heart attack, on a quiet midday afternoon, Dr. Purdy, the doctor assigned to me, knocked on my door. I was propped up in bed eating a tapioca pudding. Sabrina was fluffing the pillows behind me, helping me adjust the bed height.

"Knock, knock," he said. "Can I come inside?"

"I didn't know you did house visits." I laughed.

"Only for my favorite patient," he said. "How are we holding up?"

"Starting to feel like my old self again."

"Good," he said. "Glad to hear it." A pause. His eyes shot over to Sabrina and then back to me. "Listen, we ran some blood tests. I found some unusual abnormalities in your blood. It might be nothing, but we want to be a hundred percent sure, so I'm gonna have my lab run some additional tests. The tests usually come back in forty-eight hours. Once we get them back, we can discuss and get you out of here. I'm sure you're anxious to get home."

I shared a look of concern with Sabrina. I thought I was in the clear, but there was always a catch. I had a sinking feeling that I might not make it out of this hospital.

"What kind of abnormalities?" Sabrina asked.

"I'd rather not speculate and cause you unnecessary worry. We'll know more after we do some more extensive tests."

After the doctor left, I was worried. Sabrina calmed my nerves.

"It's just routine tests to make sure you are good before they let you escape," she said, while slapping my hand.

Visiting hours ended at five. Hospital rules didn't apply to Sabrina. She stayed by my side day and night while I recovered. The nurses didn't dare ask her to leave. She called my kids and friends to tell them the news. She assured them I was fine. My kids stopped by to check on their old man. Donnie Cooper showed his face, brought me some crossword puzzles to help pass the time. Night three and I got another visit from a friend I hadn't seen in many years—good old Sam Schwartz, one of my best and oldest friends from the Bluffs. At that point, Sam and I had been friends for forty-five years. I hadn't seen Sam in a few years, but it meant the world for him to stop by and check on me. I always kept up with the guys from the old neighborhood. In the years that had passed, Sam had become a hotshot businessman. But he never forgot his roots or the guys he grew up with. That was the thing about growing up in the Bluffs— your friends were your family. We could go years without speaking, but we'd always pick up like we hadn't missed a beat. He knocked on the door and peeked inside.

"Don't you have to have a heart to have a heart attack?" he asked.

I gave him the finger. "Always bustin' balls," I said, shaking my head.

Truth was, I envied Sam. He was the smartest guy I knew, making money hand over fist, and was married to the same woman for twentysomething years. But there was something else. It wasn't just his money or marriage that I envied. He seemed happy. He seemed at peace with the world around him. Lying in a hospital bed forces you to reexamine your life. How many times had I come face-to-face with death? How much of my life had I lost to being angry? Hours lost to fantasies of getting even. Where did it get me? What did all of this anger and hatred amount to? If the decisions I made led me to this hospital bed, what good were the decisions?

Sam stayed for an hour, and we shot the shit. But all the while, I grew envious of the calmness I felt in his presence. He stood to leave. Kissed Sabrina goodbye. Told me to give my kids a hug from him. But just before he left, I got the nerve to ask him a question. I said, "Sammy? How is it that you always seem so damn happy?"

What he told me changed my life forever: he said he had been practicing the Baha'i faith. I had never heard of the Baha'i faith. Frankly, when he said his happiness was the result of his faith, I sort of rolled my eyes. I was never much of a spiritual person. Never believed much in God. Matter of fact, I spent most of my life recruiting for the other guy. Sabrina always tried to get me to pray with her, attend church with her. I tended to mock things I didn't understand. All talk of religion made me zone out. Shut down. I didn't like being preached to and I certainly didn't want to hear it now, lying in a paper gown with two stints in my heart.

He asked me if he could share a bit about the Baha'i faith with me. I winced and shook my head no.

"C'mon, Aiden, hear me out. You got something else better to do today?"

I looked over at Sabrina with an unamused look on my face.

"You trying to convert me to a cult?" I asked him.

He laughed. He began to explain a bit about how the Baha'i faith worked. He may as well have been speaking Greek—but a few things he said got through my stubborn resistance. The Baha'i faith is the world's newest religion, he said. The second-newest religion is Islam. The faith focuses on the teachings of Bahá'u'llá—God's divine messenger—who teaches about the oneness of God and the harmonious coming together of humanity. Maybe it's because I had almost just died, but I felt tears welling in my eyes as he spoke. I had spent so much of my life disconnected from other people. Hurting other people. Hurting myself. I suddenly found a comfort in believing in something greater than myself.

Still, I resisted.

"I think I'm a lost cause," I said. "I know where I'm going after I die."

"No, you don't," he said. "Nobody knows. But if you're ever interested in forgiving yourself, let me know. You might find a community waiting to embrace you."

Sam didn't lecture me too long. Instead, he left some literature about the Baha'i faith on the table beside me. But before he left, he shared a quote that rang so true to me, I felt it deep in my soul.

"The sinner, when his heart is free from all save God, must seek forgiveness from God alone. Confession before the servants is not permissible, for it is not the means or the cause of Divine Forgiveness. The sinner must, between himself and God, beg for mercy from the Sea of Mercy and implore pardon from the Heaven of Forgiveness."

The next night, the nurse pushed my wheelchair down a crowded white hall and parked me in a cold exam room. She turned on the light and prepped the MRI. My stomach turned at the stink of hospital gauze. I wanted to go home. I wanted to start over. She took my temperature and blood pressure and jotted some notes. Then she helped me stand. Eased me onto the scanner bed.

We were on the third floor of a hospital tower just outside Newark. I had just turned fifty-six. She told me to be still. I asked her if it would hurt at all. She said no. She said I wouldn't feel a thing. I lay there in a paper gown, counting backward from ten. I kept my eyes shut tight, but my mind was in a panic. It all started coming back up. The past. Weighing on my conscience like a violent debt. One I was about to repay. The nurse pushed a red button, and I disappeared into the tube. I spent two days waiting on the results. The doctor called the house while Sabrina was at the store. We drove together to the clinic at noon the next day. I sat across from the doctor in a windowless room. His desk was a mess of paperwork and medical books. He placed a black-and-white MRI scan in front of me and said three little letters that slugged me in the sternum: A—L—S.

"Lou Gehrig's . . . " I said. He nodded to confirm my worst fears.

Time seemed to slow down as he explained my doomed future. His words came out warped, like a record spun in reverse. Like a distant radio signal. I didn't have the money to get sick. I imagined myself, helpless in a wheelchair. Unable to move. I was afraid I'd get dementia and forget Sabrina's name. I was afraid I'd forget the names of my children.

"How long do I have? To live?"

"It's hard to say," he said. "The disease affects everyone differently. I've had clients live ten, fifteen years. Others . . . months."

I left the hospital with Sabrina. Stared out the window. It was mid-December. I didn't feel like talking. Minutes passed slow. I could feel my body collapsing. This was it. I had escaped death before. Too many times to count. But it found me in the suburbs as a married man. And not in the way I thought it would. Not a bullet to the head or a knife in the back. ALS was an invisible killer. Patient and methodical. That scared me more than twenty guys with machetes.

Finally, I spoke.

"How am I gonna tell the boys?"

"We'll do it together," she said. "I'll be right there the whole time. Beside you."

"I thought I paid my debt," I said.

"What debt?"

"To God. I thought we were square. That it was over. But here He is. Back again. To collect."

"It isn't your fault that you're sick, Aiden."

"You know the worst part? I know I deserve this. For what I did."

She pulled the car over to the shoulder and clicked on her hazards. She grabbed my cold hand and held it in hers. Cars sped by us as we idled on the side of the freeway.

"You were a kid, Aiden. Why are you so quick to blame yourself?"

We drove home in silence. It was already night by the time we got there. I undressed for bed. The news of the disease had left me in shock. How was I going to tell my children?

Sabrina changed into her nightgown and climbed into bed.

"You're gonna be okay," she said. She was always an optimist. She was trying to be strong for the both of us. She could tell I was shaking. I couldn't tell if it was the cold or the nerves or the fear or the sadness. But something was making me shiver.

She took my hand in hers. "You have a lotta years left," she said. "And we're gonna make the best of them."

I closed my eyes.

"You asked me why I was so quick to blame myself," I said. "You don't know who I am or the things I've done."

"Aiden, we've been together seven years. I think I know."

"You don't," I said.

"It does not matter what you have done. I love you for you."

I clicked off the lamp. I came clean in the dark. She knew small snippets about my past, but she didn't know the full extent of the life I had led. I'd been lying to people so long—lying to myself so long—that I didn't know if I even knew the truth anymore. I shut my eyes and bared my soul to the woman I loved. I was ready to lose her. I was prepared to wake up alone in that bed. I figured once she heard about the hideous acts I'd committed, she would run and never look back. But she didn't run. She listened. And as the stories turned gruesome, she clasped my hand even tighter. I rested my head on her shoulder and told her the story of the man I was, the man I became, and the man I wanted to be. She listened and didn't say a word.

In the morning, she was still there. And I may have been given a death sentence, but I also felt alive for the first time.

The heart attack opened my eyes. ALS propelled me into action. Life was short. The clock was ticking. God had a cruel sense of humor, didn't He? In Sabrina, I had finally found a reason to live, and now He'd cursed me with a disease that was guaranteed to cut that life short. But instead of feeling sorry for myself, I decided I was going to make the most of the time I had left. So, I started doing something I'd never done before. I began mending bridges.

The first was my father. With the clock ticking on my life, I called the old man and finally put an end to our stubborn estrangement. We spent hours on the phone, hashing out our problems, forgiving each other, and making amends. We couldn't get back the years we had lost, but we still had time to make memories together.

"Why don't we all go on a cruise?" he finally said. "You, me, and Sabrina. It'll give me a chance to spend some quality time with the woman you love. And it'll give us a chance to talk."

I was hesitant at first but then a light bulb went off in my head: I would propose to Sabrina on the cruise. It would be the big, romantic gesture she deserved. She would never see it coming.

"What do you say?" my dad asked.

"Let's do it."

───────────

I bought Sabrina an engagement ring about a year after we met. Truth was, I was ready to marry her the first day I laid eyes on her.

The plan was to propose on the cruise. Hiding the ring was a chore; Sabrina packed our bags. She was a skilled, diligent, anal-retentive packer. I couldn't hide it in the luggage. I had to be creative and find a place she would never check.

Morning. The ship set sail at half past nine. The Royal Caribbean ship was a seven-decker monolith jutting out of the water. A small city of seven thousand people. Restaurants, casinos, bars, salons, shopping, swimming, gyms, and libraries. You name it, they had it. It was a consumer paradise. A place to eat and drink and numb yourself into a new reality. You could fit most of the people who lived in the Bluffs on this ship. It was good to get away. It was good to feel anonymous. The pool deck was full of pasty, potbellied men. Nine-to-five yes-men wearing shell necklaces and unbuttoned Hawaiian shirts. Their bottle-blonde wives baked beside them in the sun. Cruises weren't my scene. I'd rather be playing darts at a dive bar. But I was overdue for a vacation. I was never one for the beach. I liked the snow and the darkness. But it was a romantic experience and I wanted to share it with Sabrina.

By day, the sun beat down on us. The pool deck was a congested Disney-level clusterfuck of Midwesterners. I wasn't crazy about the crowds. Sabrina applied sunscreen to my back and face. She was always taking care of me. At night, the crowds thinned out, and Sabrina and I had time to ourselves to enjoy the peaceful night air. The white moon haloed above, and the sound of the crashing waves brought a sense of serenity I had never before experienced.

Still, as the ship departed Fort Lauderdale and headed toward the Virgin Islands, my stomach was in knots. It was an excited kind of nervousness. I was poised to propose to the woman I loved. I needed the proposal to go smoothly. No hiccups, no fuckups. I just wanted one thing in my life to go right. I needed Sabrina to know how special she was to me. So, I tried my best to choreograph it. That first night, after Sabrina turned in for bed inside our small, ocean-view cabin, I met with the manager of the cruise ship's most upscale restaurant. I told him the plan.

"You want me to hide this ring in one of our desserts?" he asked.

"I'll order the chocolate soufflé. You just set the ring on top, like a cherry. Just right there on top of the cake." I removed the ring box from my pocket and palmed it inside his hand.

"Lose this ring and they'll find you floating in the Atlantic," I said. "Got it?"

He swallowed hard. "Got it."

Except he didn't get shit. Night three on the ship and I dressed in the nicest suit I had. Sabrina, my father, and I had a decadent steak and lobster dinner. A lounge singer crooned next to a white piano. But when the dessert came out—the chocolate soufflé—there was no ring anywhere.

Oh fuck, I thought. They lost the ring. I started to panic. Sabrina looked at me. I smiled like nothing was wrong. Just stay calm, I told myself.

When she reached the bottom of her chocolate soufflé, her fork hit something that made a metallic clink. It wasn't the plate. The dessert chef must've hid the ring inside the soufflé. What a dipshit, I thought. But still, the moment had arrived. I looked at Sabrina, who looked at me. Then back to the plate. My heart began to race. I had been confident she would say yes, but in the moment, I started to second-guess myself. She scraped some more chocolate up and the ring came into view.

She picked up the ring and studied it. Light refracted in the diamond's ridges. She cupped her hand over her mouth. She stood and backed away. I stood, too, and took her by the hand. I took a knee and a deep breath.

"Aiden . . . " she said.

"I've been ready to propose to you since the first moment I laid eyes on you. You're the only person in the world I want to spend the rest of my life with. Would you do me the honor of being my wife?"

I could see tears welling in her eyes. She sniffled away her tears. She didn't answer at first. She just stood there trying to make sense of what was happening. All around us, people were staring, some with their cell phones out, taking a video. And then, after a long pause, she finally answered.

"Can I think about it?" she said. And then she broke into a big smile.

That was our sense of humor. She was always breaking my balls and I loved her for it. Before I even had a chance to answer, she said, "Of course I'll marry you."

My father, along with the other diners, erupted into applause. I stood and embraced my future wife. After nearly a decade of being together, I was finally going to make my best friend and soulmate my wife.

The rest of the week whizzed by. On the last night of the cruise, I made time to catch up with my father. My father said meet me at seven. I threw on a button-down and took the elevator down. The bar on three was a dark martini lounge. The bar was dim, quivering in candlelight. He was standing at a polished marble high-top. He threw back a whiskey and ordered another. I hugged him close. He was drenched in cologne and aftershave. His mood was off-kilter.

The bar windows looked out onto a pitch-black ocean. Moonlight reflected off the water. We made some polite small talk. I had the feeling he needed to get something off his chest. Then finally he said, "Your mom would've loved this." It was the first time I heard him talk about her since she got sick. My parents rarely went on vacation. They grew up in the Depression and hoarded their money.

"Haven't heard you mention Mom in a while," I said.

"Not an easy subject for me," he said.

"Maybe you feel guilty for the way you left things," I said.

"Maybe there are things you don't know about your mother."

"What are you talking about?"

The question hung in the tension, just like that day at the bar in Bradenton. I'd had enough of his cryptic messages. It was time to come clean.

My father waves down the waiter. Ordered a Scotch, neat. He nursed his drink while he took a deep breath.

"What I'm gonna tell you about your mother stays between us," he said. "She swore me to secrecy, and for fifty years I've never told another living soul."

"Are you being serious?" I asked.

He nodded. His face was somber in a way I hadn't seen for years. "Your mother was born a Hungarian Jew," he said.

My mind flashed back to my mom's words as she lay dying. At the time, I thought it was just gibberish from a dying woman who had lost touch with reality. Now, at fifty-six, for the first time in my life, I found out that my mom was a Jew.

"Her Jewish faith was something she was forced to hide. Forced to abandon. She did it for survival."

I dragged my hands over my face.

"What are you saying?"

He downed his Scotch and began to explain a horror I never could've imagined. I closed my eyes and let his agonizing words wash over me.

It was 1945. My mother was eleven years old, living in a tenement in Buda, north of the Danube River. The Nazis had been defeated. The Russians were invading. Military tanks went rumbling through the streets. Red stars on every corner. Gaslight lamps lit the streets in muddled yellow. The city was in shambles. Ruinous heaps of rubble. Historic houses, churches, theaters, and bridges decimated by Allied bombs. And the Russians were like vultures, rolling into town, wolves in sheep's clothing, come to pick the bones of the vulnerable Hungarians.

I squinted as my father took a sharp shot of whiskey and continued on with the story. From his own lips, he shared a harrowing story of my mother during the Soviet invasion. It was the story of a young girl who witnessed these savage Russian soldiers break into her house, rifles in hand, drunk and belligerent, ransacking their bedrooms, brutalizing her father, who tried to stand up for his family. They were emboldened by victory, keyed up on drugs and vodka. They were bloodthirsty soldiers looking for women to bully, rape, and murder. My mother happened to be in their firing line.

Rage rushed through my body as my father shared the sordid details. My mind flashed back to my mother on her deathbed, crying in terror, trying to warn me that the Russians were coming. It hadn't made any sense then, but now, hearing the tremble in my father's voice, I realized it wasn't a hallucination. It was my mother's deepest fears resurfacing in the final moments of her life.

My father swallowed hard. His voice began cracking as he told me a story from my mother's past that had been hidden her entire life: the Russian soldiers threw my mother down and repeatedly raped her. It was a violent and vulgar assault on a little girl who ceased to exist that night. Somehow, she survived the horror of those rapes. She spent months in the hospital, my father said, pissing blood for weeks. Her face swollen and bruised and unrecognizable. The person who emerged from those rapes was not the same little girl. The person was a woman who was forced to numb herself to survive an unspeakable trauma.

After my mother recovered, she joined an underground network of resistance fighters with my father. She was twelve years old—the same age I was when I joined the Mafia. My mother wanted revenge for what they did to her and her family. The resistance fighters taught her to fight. They trained her to be a killer. They trained her how to use an ice pick to kill people.

I put up my hand and stopped my father.

"Did you say an ice pick?"

He nodded.

An ice pick was the weapon I wielded when I would protect Eddy Tocio. It was as if I unknowingly inherited my numbness and violence from my mother.

"Dad, Mom mentioned something about being Jewish before she died."

"Yeah, Mom kept that hidden."

More than six hundred thousand Hungarian Jews were led to slaughter by the Nazis during World War II. After the war, the Soviets entered Hungary, first as allies, but they quickly turned to enemies, who performed acts of unspeakable cruelty against the citizens. But my mother refused to go quietly. She wasn't about to sit idly by while the Soviets abused her and her people. She was responsible for killing more than sixty Soviet soldiers.

As my father told this harrowing story, I felt like I was trapped in a bad dream. How could I not have known? My mother was my best friend. She was my entire life. She was the woman I loved more than anything on Earth. I would've killed for her. How could she not have told me? Did she think she was protecting me?

Tears dripped down my face into the crevices of my mouth.

My father set his hand gently on my wrist.

"Your mother killed to survive. She numbed herself against the horrors she endured. She was never the same after that. I'm not sure she ever allowed herself to feel again. Leaving your mother was the hardest thing I ever did," he said. "But I wasn't strong enough to deal with the pain she was struggling with. I wish I was, but I wasn't. And I just wanted to say I'm sorry, Aiden. I'm sorry I walked out on her. And I'm sorry she had to endure all she did."

I wiped the tears from my face with my forearm. After all these years in the dark, I finally understood why my father left the marriage. The trauma my mother experienced left her numb. She was a survivor, but she had so much difficulty accepting love. It must've felt impossible for my father to get close to her. And while she was capable of showing incredible warmth toward me, she struggled to find that same love for him. It was so easy to blame him. But I never knew the whole story.

"Why didn't anybody tell me?"

"We thought we were protecting you," he said.

My entire life I was never able to feel. Doctors had told me I lacked empathy. I had spent years trying to understand why I had this sadistic streak in me. I had never been able to feel for other people. Even when I hurt someone else, I felt a blankness inside that I couldn't describe. Now, sitting there in that martini lounge, I wondered if I inherited that trait from my mother. She had suffered such unspeakable horrors, and the scale of the murders she committed were incomprehensible. At some point during her young life, she must've learned to shut off her emotions so she could kill without feeling. Could I have inherited her callousness?

Was it possible to endure such horror that the numbness you feel can be passed on to your children? Was it possible my capacity for inflicting pain was something I'd gotten from her?

For the first time in nearly twenty years, I hugged my father. Then, without saying a word, I walked back to my cabin, where Sabrina was waiting for me. She must've sensed in my silence that something was wrong.

"Everything all right?" she asked.

"Just ready to go home," I said. "Just ready to get married and begin our life. I'm just ready to start over."

"Are you sure you are okay? If something is bothering you, you have to get it out. If not with me, then with someone."

"I am all right, babe, just overwhelmed with everything. I cannot wait to start our life together."

That night I lay awake, reliving the story my dad told me. Little things started falling into place. Mom never did like going to church. She always was quick to defend and never afraid to get into someone's face. Mom always wanted to take care of everyone around her. She always stressed the importance of family. Now things were making sense.

CHAPTER 16

The wedding was an intimate affair. Small, tasteful. Tucked away in the woods of rural Jersey. Rain clouds brewed in the sky above the chapel. We interpreted the drizzle as a sign of good luck from the gods. It was more than a wedding; it was a culmination of a life. It was a gathering of every important person I'd ever met—neighborhood kids from the Bluffs, guys from the police force, and loved ones from Sabrina's family. Past and present, it was a day acknowledging the past and celebrating the future. I wore a black tux. She wore a white gown. My son Nolan was my best man. My other son Chris was in the wedding party along with my best friends Sam Schwartz and Donnie Cooper.

Sabrina and I wrote our own vows. I vowed to be a man worthy of her love. She vowed to always stand by my side. Even before God, she busted my balls and had the audience in stitches. We even included some lines from *Family Guy*, a show that shared our sense of humor. We danced and drank and smushed handfuls of wedding cake into each other's faces. Later, as the wedding waned, Sam said a Baha'i prayer. He acknowledged that the Baha'i calendar states that "Love" is the name given to the tenth year in each Baha'i cycle of nineteen years. Sabrina and I had been together for a decade. After that, he said a quiet prayer. I held Sabrina's hands in mine as he spoke.

"O my Lord! O my Lord! These two bright orbs are wedded in Thy love. Conjoined in servitude to Thy holy threshold. United in ministering to Thy cause. Make Thou this marriage to be as threading lights of Thine abounding grace. O my Lord, the All-Merciful, and luminous rays of Thy bestowals. O Thou the Beneficent, the Ever Giving, that there may branch out from this great tree boughs that will grow green and flourishing through the gifts that rain down from Thy clouds of grace."

The fuss and the commotion of the wedding concluded. Sabrina and I returned to our quiet suburban lives. Some days later, the kids were set to come over for dinner. As we prepared the meal that night, a warm sense of gratitude washed over me.

Somehow, after all the mistakes I had made and all the obstacles God had thrown at me, I had ended up with a family that loved me. I had spent my entire life trying to piece together a family. Whether it was the Mafia, or football teams, or the police force, or even with Carrie, I had so desperately wanted to be part of something. I had love to give. I wanted to feel needed. I wanted to connect with others. I didn't want to feel disposable ever again. But after so many years of trying, it was something I accepted that maybe, just maybe, love just wasn't in the cards for me. But as I looked around my kitchen that night, standing beside my brand-new bride, I realized that I ended up exactly where I was always meant to be. Every choice I had ever made led me there, to that moment. And as rocky as the road had been, I wouldn't change a thing.

That night, after hearing me talk to the kids about my newfound gratitude, Sabrina made one final request. She wanted me to give the Baha'i faith a chance.

I resisted.

"Ah, c'mon," I said. "I've never been a religious person."

But she insisted. Sabrina knew how much I loved and respected my friend Sam. She thought it would be good for me. I knew her well enough to know she wouldn't lead me astray. The hard truth was that death changes people. I had lived my entire life pretending I was invincible. But I wasn't. It had all caught up with me. It was time to pay my debt and I was scared. I knew what was coming for me.

We rarely spoke about the dark days that loomed. We chose to speak about hope. Not about the years I would miss but all the days I had left. But the ALS would progress. It would slowly snuff out hope. My health would deteriorate. I'd lose control of my faculties. I'd slowly begin to disappear. We both knew the agonizing road that awaited me. I was scared and she saw it in my eyes. I needed something to believe in.

The Baha'i meetings were held on Tuesdays. I knew the basics from Sam. A small part of me wished I could leave my cynicism behind and embrace a faith. But I was a cold, callous guy. I felt I had seen and endured too much to believe in God again. I reluctantly joined the Zoom call. Seven other faces popped up on the screen. I introduced myself. It was all wrong. I didn't belong here. They all seemed so normal. None of these people were ever scarred up and riddled with bullet holes. None of them had ever stared down the barrel of a gun. None of them had shoved a man's head in a vise for a Mafia underboss. These were happy people with normal problems. What could I possibly have in common with any of them?

Since I was the newest member to the prayer group, the session leader, Jessica, addressed me directly. "Aiden, we begin every meeting with a prayer. Because this is your first session, you're welcome to listen in."

Then she shut her eyes and began: "O, son of being! Bring thyself to account each day thou art summoned to a reckoning; for death, unheralded, shall come upon thee and thou shalt be called to give account for thy deeds."

My instinct was to crack a joke. That's what I always did when I felt uncomfortable. I felt ridiculous. I felt like an imposter. I stayed quiet that first session. I didn't have anything to add. I was too embarrassed to talk.

But something else happened that day. I felt the smallest shift occurring inside me. Throughout the session, I learned a bit about each of those on the call who had declared for the Baha'i faith. What I took away was that everyone had been through their own struggles. Each of them needed this faith in their own way. I was skeptical, but I was moved. As the first session ended, they closed with a prayer.

"In the hearts of men, no real love is found. And the condition is such that, unless their susceptibilities are quickened by some power is that unity, love and accord may develop within them, there can be no healing."

No healing, I thought to myself. The session ended and I exited the call.

"How'd it go?" Sabrina said.

"Eh, I don't think it's for me," I said. "I think it's too late for me to start believing in this stuff."

Sabrina stared at me from across the room.

"But you'll keep trying?"

"C'mon, what's the point?"

"Aiden, you promised me."

"I felt so embarrassed listening to them saying their prayers. That's not who I am."

"Just go one more time," she said. "For me."

On the next Zoom session, Sabrina decided to join me. I think it was her way of making sure I followed through with my promise. This time, I felt an unexpected approachability toward the others in the group. Their stories, their lives inspired me. I never went to AA meetings when I was drinking, but I imagined it felt similar to this. The camaraderie made me feel less alone. So in the final moments of the session, I decided to open up about my ALS. The group fell quiet as I shared my darkest fears and the hopelessness I was feeling. It was an uncharacteristic moment of vulnerability for me. I felt naked as I bared my soul to this group of strangers. Sabrina held my hand and encouraged me along.

But I needed to tell someone outside of my family. With my Baha'i group, I found a safe place where I didn't have to be strong. I could just be me. As I finished spilling my guts to the group, the session leader thanked me for sharing. Then she shared a quote from Baha'u'llah.

"Set all thy hope in God and cleave tenaciously to His unfailing mercy. Who else but Him can enrich the destitute, and deliver the fallen from his abasement?"

I was trying. Something remained in the way. The prayers I said felt performative. I didn't feel like I was connecting to the faith the way the others did. I continued to go to the prayer meetings. Week after week, I tried. I said the words, but I wasn't sure I felt anything. Maybe I was incapable of feeling. I wasn't sure. Sabrina and I would discuss the meetings and the information we learned. Always encouraging me and pushing me when I wanted to skip a meeting. I slowly found myself liking some of the ideals of the Baha'i faith, sharing those with Sabrina, and collaborating with her on the readings.

I was never much of a reader, but I started reading some Baha'i books that Sam recommended. One book in particular stood out to me. In was a book called *Post Traumatic Slave Syndrome* by a Baha'i named Dr. Joy DeGruy. In her book, she talks about the residual impacts of generations of slavery upon the Black community. As a policeman, I had seen the results of this trauma up close and personal. As I read the book, for the first time, I began to understand the effect of my own family's trauma, trauma I had no idea about for most of my life. It made me understand even more about the oneness of humanity, how every family has its own trauma and tragedy that they are coming to grips with. With every page, I began to see a clearer picture of my mom as a young girl struggling to survive and deal with the anger of the terrible crime she endured and how she had to shut off her emotions to protect herself. And that anger got passed on to me. Finally, after many decades of wandering, with the help of an amazing woman named Sabrina and the healing Baha'i prayers, I was slowly finding my way home.

About four months after I began with the prayer group, I began suffering some of the side effects of my ALS medication. And that's when something unexplainable happened. I started feeling the presence of my deceased mother in my life. Each night, I'd feel her aura, her spirit. Sometimes I would even smell her perfume. I was too shy to bring it up in the prayer group, but after sharing it all with Sabrina, I summoned the courage to mention my experience. The reaction I received was what made me a believer.

I thought they were going to laugh at me, but they didn't. They listened patiently and kindly to my story. It was Sammy who finally spoke when I was done.

He spoke about how the Baha'i faith rejects reincarnation. Instead, they believe the soul is ever progressing, through spiritual worlds. His words gave me comfort, a comfort I had been looking for for a long, long time. I wanted to believe my mother was doing exactly that. And that one day, after I died, that I, too, would be soaring right beside her. The two of us together. Flying through the spiritual worlds, finally at peace. That's where I wanted to spend eternity. It was that moment I decided to let go of my cynicism and surrender to the Baha'i faith.

CHAPTER 17

On the day I declared, Sabrina and I drove to a Baha'i member's home for my ceremony. Inside, I was greeted by my friend Sam and dozens of Baha'i from the area spiritual assembly. I felt barbaric among these poised and civil people. The preppy men with their turtlenecks with white-collar jobs. They sat clutching the hands of their wives, who were dressed immaculately in pantsuits and strings of pearls. And then there was me: disheveled, unsophisticated, and inarticulate me. The gangster from the Bluffs. Walking into a prayer group with a limp because I still had shrapnel in my leg.

I squeezed Sabrina's hand. I was happy she was standing beside me. She had been with me on this spiritual journey. Always encouraging, listening, helping me understand this spiritual world and of course kicking my butt when I was being stubborn.

They all welcomed me with a hug. Because just like Sabrina, they didn't see the man I was. They saw the man I would become.

Sam smiled and began the simple ceremony.

"Aiden, I know this has been a journey. A journey you never thought you would make, but here you are. I am proud that you allowed me to be part of this journey with you. If we would have only known about the Baha'i faith forty-five years ago when we were kids, maybe our paths would have been different. But it does not matter about the past, as we are here today. Today you have opened your soul to the faith."

The ceremony consisted of each member reading their favorite prayer or reading from the Book. Everyone went around the room and explained why it was their favorite and then proceeded reading. They expressed their love for the faith and why they declared at different points in their lives.

It was now my turn to declare my faith.

"I bear witness, O my God, that Thou has created me to know Thee and to worship Thee. I testify, at this moment, to my powerlessness and to Thy might, to my poverty and to Thy wealth. There is none other God but Thee, the Help in Peril, the Self-Subsisting."

As the words left my lips, tears ran down my face. I thought about the young man I was—so violent, so cold. I thought about all the years I spent unable to feel. Now I was feeling everything. I was ready to begin my journey toward forgiveness. To leave the past in the past. And to spend the rest of my days trying to do better. I surrendered myself to God. I stood and opened my eyes. The group applauded and welcomed me into the family. I was never afraid to die. But now, for the first time, I wasn't afraid to live.

POSTSCRIPT

"Divine civilization, however, so traineth every member of society that no one, with the exception of a negligible few, will undertake to commit a crime. There is thus a great difference between the prevention of crime through measures that are violent and retaliatory, and so training the people, and enlightening them, and spiritualizing them, that without any fear of punishment or vengeance to come, they will shun all criminal acts. They will, indeed, look upon the very commission of a crime as a great disgrace and in itself the harshest of punishments. They will become enamoured of human perfections, and will consecrate their lives to whatever will bring light to the world and will further those qualities which are acceptable at the Holy Threshold of God."

—'Abdu'l-Bahá, *Selections from the Writings of 'Abdu'l-Bahá*

ACKNOWLEDGMENTS

I would like to start off by giving credit to two people who made this book more readable than it otherwise might have been: my loving wife and writer Kenny Porpora. Thank you, Kenny, for compiling my fading memories and turning my crazy life into this book. My wife for listening to me endlessly drone on and on and for helping keep me on track in order to get this completed. Without the two of you this would just be a jumble of words.

I owe an enormous debt to my good friend Sam for believing in me and this book. I appreciate you pushing me into this journey and being there along the way as a great supporter throughout the years.

Thank you to my family and friends for sticking with me through thick and thin. It has been truly a bumpy ride, but I have finally found Love and Peace.

I am immensely grateful to Kevin Anderson & Associates and Skyhorse Publishing for their continued support and guidance.

Of course life is not possible without the love of God, and I am thankful that I have finally found faith.

My God, my Adored One, my King, my Desire! What tongue can voice my thanks to Thee? I was heedless, Thou didst awaken me. I had turned back from Thee, Thou didst graciously aid me to turn towards Thee. I was as one dead, Thou didst quicken me with the water of life. I was withered, Thou didst revive me with the heavenly stream of Thine utterance which hath flowed forth from the pen of the All-Merciful. O Divine Providence! All existence is begotten by Thy bounty; deprive it not of the waters of Thy generosity, neither do Thou withhold it from the ocean of Thy mercy. I beseech Thee to aid and assist me at all times and under all conditions, and seek from the heaven of Thy grace Thine ancient favor. Thou art, in truth, the Lord of bounty, and the Sovereign of the kingdom of eternity.

—Bahá'u'lláh, *Prayers and Meditations by Bahá'u'lláh*